Christian Celebrations for

Passover

*Worship Outlines for
Families and Congregations*

Restoration Foundation

Restoration Foundation is an international, transdenominational, multicultural teaching and publishing resource to the Christian community. This ministry features a network of scholars, church leaders, and laypersons who share the vision for restoring the Hebrew foundations of the Christian faith, promoting the unity of the Spirit among believers, and returning the church to a biblical relationship of loving support for the international Jewish community and the nation of Israel.

We publish *Restore!* magazine, a high-quality journal that features theological balance and scholarly research. *Restore!* helps Christians recover their Hebraic heritage while strengthening their faith in Jesus. We also publish and distribute *Golden Key Books*, a publishing effort that focuses exclusively on producing and marketing books and other materials that teach the various aspects of Christianity's Jewish roots.

We maintain an inspirational and informative Internet web site: www.restorationfoundation.org. Through this medium, we make much of our material available free of charge to people around the world. Entire issues of *Restore!* and volumes of *Golden Key Books* can be studied here.

We are pleased to offer to all denominations and fellowships the teaching of our gifted scholars for conferences, seminars, and other instructional forums that can be tailored to each individual setting.

Our team of *Golden Key Partners* around the world help us translate these various parts of our expansive vision into the programs that touch the lives of thousands. We invite you to join us as full partners in this teaching and publishing ministry. Together we are making a difference in the world by restoring Christians to their biblically Hebraic heritage, by eradicating Judaeophobia and anti-Semitism, by supporting Israel and the international Jewish community, and by encouraging unity among those who share this vision.

For information about Restoration Foundation, *Restore!* magazine, *Golden Key Books*, *Living Emblems*, *Beth Midrash*, conference speakers, and *Golden Key Partnerships*, contact us at the address below.

Restoration Foundation
P. O. Box 421218
Atlanta, Georgia 30342, U.S.A.
www.RestorationFoundation.org

Christian Celebrations for

Passover

Worship Outlines for
Families and Congregations

Compiled and Edited by
John D. Garr, Ph.D., Th.D.

GOLDEN KEY BOOKS
Let Us Observe the Festival Series
Restoration Foundation
P. O. Box 421218
Atlanta, Georgia 30342, U.S.A.

TABLE OF CONTENTS

Christians
and Passover

In Leviticus 23, God himself enumerated what he called, "*my feasts*," and then enjoined their observance upon his chosen people forever. From this action alone, it is clear that God supports and sponsors celebration. The very Hebrew word translated "festival" reveals its purpose. *Chag* (from *chagag*) means to dance or twirl in a circle in ecstatic joy. No somber, ominous, morose, lachrymose events, these divinely ordained festivals! While the gods of the pagans kept their subjects in fear and torment, dreading some capricious, vengeful act of retribution, the Eternal has always expected his subjects to be filled with joy whenever they have assembled with him during his convocations.

The unbridled, God-intoxicated emotion of the Jewish people in their ecstatic worship of God continued into the earliest church, as is evidenced by the recorded events of the first Pentecost following Christ's ascension. These Jews—Jesus and his apostles—were able to celebrate the goodness of God's provision, for they understood that everything God had created was divinely "good." Passover for them was not a sad, foreboding exercise, but rather a joyous celebration.

As the church became increasingly Gentile, however, political, social, and religious pressures gradually diminished its Hebrew consciousness, replacing it with Greek rationalism. Days and seasons were changed to accommodate nationalist sensibilities. God's holy days were sacrificed in favor of man's appointed celebrations. A rich legacy of biblical tradition was soon buried under the encroaching sands of human tradition, depriving millions of Christians of their biblical heritage. The seasonal clarion calls of remembrance of God's mighty acts were silenced. Rich symbolism that ever clarified mature relationships with God faded into oblivion. Christians came to be impoverished, deprived of clear pictures of the living Christ that for centuries had been painted annually in the chosen festivals of the Hebrew Scriptures.

The good news is that God will ever labor to restore what is important to his plan for man. And nothing could be more essential to the Almighty than a growing, mature, ongoing relationship of loving devotion with his chosen people. It is for this reason that the Holy Spirit has moved to bring about a restoration of God's appointment calendar so that his people may meet with him on his appointed days.

The words of the earliest apostle to the Gentiles now echo and resonate in the hearts of millions of believers worldwide: "Christ our Passover is sacrificed for us; therefore, let us observe the festival . . . with the unleavened bread of sincerity and truth" (1 Corinthians 5:7-8). God's festivals are pregnant with meaning for those who embrace them, and they open the door to intimacy with the Divine at his appointed times. Observing them neither secures nor maintains one's status with God. Righteousness is by grace through faith only in the shed blood of Jesus. Worship, however, should be that which is done in Spirit and in truth, carried out in the focused intensity of the Holy Spirit and in the accuracy and order of the revealed Word of God.

In this book, we will offer worship outlines designed to include both Jewish orders and language as well as Christian form and tradition. Any of these may be modified, expanded, or condensed. The purpose is to help Christian families and congregations celebrate Passover in a manner consistent with the observance that Jesus and the earliest Jewish and Gentile Christians enjoyed in manners that will accommodate their own Christian understanding and tradition.

First, a complete Passover Haggadah will be offered, including the various features that have long been common to Jewish Passover observance. This *seder* (order) contains various traditional blessings which are given in Hebrew with transliterations and in English. The leader may choose to omit the Hebrew, using the English translations instead.

Second, we will offer a commentary and a Passover Haggadah that is limited to the elements of the traditional Jewish Passover Seder which we know Jesus and the apostles observed when they celebrated the Last Supper. This is an abbreviated version of the complete Passover Haggadah which will be more easily celebrated in a traditional Christian corporate worshiping setting where time constraints would make the traditional Seder seem laborious and time-consuming.

Third, we will offer as a New Covenant Passover celebration a Liturgy for Holy Communion. This ceremony will feature some elements of the synagogue liturgy that was a part of the life experience of both Jesus and the apostles during the first century of the common era. It will also feature language commonly used in that time for blessings, including the blessing to God for the elements of communion, the bread and the fruit of the vine. This Liturgy for Holy Communion can be used in any congregational setting, especially those of sacramental communions and fellowships.

I would like to express my personal thanks to my colleagues Dr. Marvin R. Wilson, Dr. Clifford Denton, Dr. Karl D. Coke, and Dwight A. Pryor for their invaluable assistance in the development and production of this book. I am also deeply indebted to Judy Grehan both for excellent input into the manuscript and for careful editing of the text. Then, my sincere appreciation goes to my friends Zvi Zachor and Yuval Shomron for their encouragement and help in the production and the marketing of this book.

Passover observance in which both the Exodus event and the Calvary experience are celebrated is foundational to Christian faith. The very first Passover is a part of Christian salvation history, a seminal event in the unbroken chain of deliverance that eventuated in the manifestation of Yeshua, the Messiah and Savior of the world. The very first Passover of the New Covenant era is most assuredly essential to Christian faith, for it was on this day that the Son of God, the Son of man, offered himself on the cross for the redemption of humanity.

Answers to the question of why Christians would want to observe Passover with traditional Jewish forms and language should be apparent. If these worship experiences were important to Jesus and his disciples (and it is beyond doubt that they were), they should certainly be of great import to those who assert that they are "like Christ" by calling themselves "Christians." The question of Passover observance for Christians, then, is not "Why?" but "Why not?"

The choice is ours. Is Passover observance essential to salvation? No! Salvation is grounded solely in our faith in Jesus; therefore, Passover observance can never been seen as a salvation exercise. It is, however, a worship exercise, an opportunity to offer pure, biblically sound praise and adoration to the heavenly Father for the unmerited gift of his unfathomable grace in sending his only begotten Son into the world that all men might be saved and inherit the gift of eternal life.

Christians are not required to observe Passover, however, they certainly have the liberty to do so. Passover is an annual appointment to remember God's redemption, first of Israel, and then of all mankind. It is an opportunity to fulfill the command of Jesus that believers "remember his death" until he returns. Because Christ our Passover has been sacrificed for us, let us, therefore, observe this festival.

Fraternally in the Messiah
John D. Garr, Ph.D., Th.D.
Hanukkah 2003

Passover: Two Miracles, Two Peoples, Two Religions

Passover is a perpetual memorial of two seminal events that are foundational to Judaism and Christianity. Each time a Torah-observant Jew or a Bible-believing Christian celebrates the Passover, he is calling to remembrance one or both of history's greatest events, the Exodus experience and the Calvary event. Without the Exodus, there would be no Jewish people. Without both the Exodus and Calvary, there would be no Christianity. As Anthony Saldarini has rightly observed, "Passover lives on in both the Jewish and Christian communities as a central ritual which expresses each community's identity and nature" (*Jesus and Passover*, p. 4).

Passover marks two of the momentous times in history when the rectilinear path of divine providence intersected the plane of human need, times when the Eternal took the sovereign initiative to solve the woefully twisted enigma of human suffering. In one divine miracle of Passover deliverance, God brought forth a nation of perhaps two million Jews from one of history's most onerous slaveries, establishing for all succeeding generations the hope of the divine imperative: "Let my people go!" In another Passover miracle, the all-loving, all-knowing Father provided his Son as a Passover Lamb whose death on the cross provided the atonement by which human sin could be passed over in love and mercy.

Immediately after the Passover event which produced Israel's Exodus from Egypt, God commanded the Israelites to celebrate the Passover each year forever (Exodus 12:14). He considered remembering the details of his miraculous deliverance so important that he established as the penalty for the nonobservance excommunication from the company of Israel and from the presence of God (Exodus 12:15). For Israel's first fifteen hundred years, both the linear descendants of Jacob's sons and the unknown multitudes of Gentiles who chose to embrace God's covenant with Israel observed the commandment.

It was entirely ordinary, then, that Jesus and his disciples shared the Passover meal in the evening before his death, and it was natural that Jesus would partake of the elements of that meal, during which he established a New Covenant Passover ritual for all those who would come to faith in his name. "No other religious ritual better reveals the organic relationship that exists between Judaism and Christianity," says Samuele Bacchiocchi, "than the Passover meal partaken of and transformed by Jesus into the very symbol of His redemption" (*God's Festivals in Scripture and History, Part 1, the Spring Festivals*, p. 32).

PASSOVER AND THE EXODUS

God commanded his chosen people to observe Passover throughout all their generations so that they might remember that their very existence as a people was wholly dependent upon his gracious act of deliverance. Every Israelite in subsequent history was to declare on each annual celebration of the Passover, "I was a slave in Egypt," maintaining the indelible impression that not only were his ancestors delivered from slavery but in a very real sense, he himself was likewise liberated. Individual freedom is not the result of an accident of history: it is the product of God's lovingkindness and the miracle of his deliverance.

The enslaved Israelites' ancestors had come to Egypt as celebrities when Joseph was so positioned by divine providence as to save not only the chosen people but all of Egypt as well. As a result of a divine gift that gave him insight into Egypt's future, Joseph was exalted by Pharaoh to be Egypt's prime minister and was given the charge of devising and implementing a plan to prepare for the seven years of famine which he foresaw and of administering the distribution of the stores of food during that time.

As time progressed, the seventy family members who came with Joseph into Egypt multiplied to the point that the Egyptian authorities began to fear the power of their numbers. A Pharaoh "who knew not Joseph" began to enslave the Israelites, forcing them to work in deplorable conditions to build the architectural wonders of Egypt.

Faced with no prospect for relief, the Israelites cried out to God for deliverance in an agonizing petition for liberation from the bitterness of their oppression. In order to underscore the miraculous provisions of his providence, God purposed to send a deliverer with a divine plan to liberate his enslaved people.

At a time when Pharaoh had ordered that all male Israelite infants be drowned in the Nile River, a resourceful daughter of Israel hid her son Moses for the first three months of his life. Then she placed the infant in a basket of reeds and with faith in God placed the boat in the Nile. The small craft floated directly to one of Pharaoh's daughters who "coincidentally" was bathing nearby.

Pharaoh's daughter immediately had compassion on the baby and adopted him as her own son. Thus, a slave baby was positioned in the imperial house where he acquired the world's best education, political power, and personal wealth. Despite the riches of Egypt that were lavished upon him by a doting stepmother, Moses could not escape his true patrimony: he was a son of the very slaves who were being exploited by Egypt.

After a time when Moses was forty years of age, his suppressed anger erupted as he witnessed one of his people being severely beaten by an Egyptian taskmaster. Enraged with indignation, he killed the taskmaster. When Moses realized that his actions had been observed, he fled to the remote Sinai desert.

For forty years Moses passed his time as a shepherd in the arid, lifeless landscape. One day as he passed the barren slopes of Mount Sinai, out of the corner of his eye he caught a glimpse of a bush that was burning (not an unusual sight in this desert of scorching heat where bushes of this type often undergo spontaneous combustion). What riveted Moses' attention to this bush was the fact that despite the intense flame that encompassed it, the bush was not consumed.

When Moses "turned aside to see" this phenomenon, he positioned himself directly in the path of God's voice that called to him, "Moses, Moses." The Eternal God commissioned Moses to return to Egypt with a fateful message for Pharaoh: "Let my people go."

Moses was not to secure Israel's liberty through his skills in diplomacy. By this time, he suffered from a "slowness of speech." He was to be equipped with divine authority to call forth miracles to attest to the divine authorship of his commands for Pharaoh. His shepherd's staff became "the rod of God" which produced many miracles.

God's plan was simple: speak to Pharaoh the words of the divine imperative and then be a channel for the display of awesome power. Ten plagues were devised by the hand of the Almighty to bring progressively more painful suffering to the land of Egypt to punish the obduracy of its leader. Interestingly, each of these plagues was also designed to demonstrate the Lord God's judgment against Egypt's gods. To the amazement of the Egyptians in particular and perhaps of even most of the children of Jacob, Goshen, the land where the enslaved Israelites lived, was spared the withering effects of some of the plagues. In Goshen, there were no swarming creatures, no dying cattle, no boils, no hail, no locusts, and no darkness.

The last of the plagues targeted the Egyptian idolatry wherein Pharaoh and his son were worshipped as incarnate deities. The firstborn of everyone in the land of Egypt was to be destroyed as the Lord himself passed through the land. The major difference between this concluding plague and its predecessors would be the fact that this time, Goshen would not escape the visitation of this night of terror.

In order to prepare the Israelites and provide a way of escape for their firstborn, God gave Moses a simple plan: on the fourteenth day of the first month, each of the families of Israel would sacrifice an unblemished lamb at the threshold of their house. In an open display of disrespect for heathen gods, the lamb was sacrificed in the basin at the threshold of the door of each home. Then, the patriarch of each family dipped a piece of hyssop in the blood at the threshold and applied it conspicuously to both doorposts and to the lintel of the door, in effect completely encircling the door with the blood. "When I see the blood," God said, "I will pass over you." The Hebrew word for "pass over" is *pesach*, which literally means "to jump over." Marking the entry to each house with blood from the "paschal" lamb provided a way of escape for the Israelite firstborn.

A second part of the requirement for escape was that the families remain in their houses throughout the night of the Passover, eating the roasted lamb, consuming bitter herbs, and sharing in bread that was made without yeast. The bread was the bread of affliction, but it was also the bread of haste. After a seemingly interminable duration of suffering in slavery, God would do a quick work to bring his people out.

The Israelites awoke the following morning to find their firstborn spared. The Egyptians, on the other hand, were devastated, for the firstborn of every house, including that of Pharaoh, had died. In desperation Pharaoh's hardened heart finally relented, and he ordered the Israelites to leave Egypt. Throughout that day, the chosen people requested and received from the Egyptians gold and silver (equivalent to wages for the time of their slavery). Then, on the fifteenth day of the first month of the year, they departed from Egypt "with a high hand," knowing that God himself had delivered them.

The route that God chose for their escape was one which brought them face to face with the Red Sea. (The term *Red Sea* is a misnomer. It is actually the Reed Sea, *Yam Suph* in Hebrew). By that time, Pharaoh had reconsidered the liberation of the Israelites and had determined to retake them. The entire camp of Israel found itself confronted by the choice of death in the Red Sea or at the hand of Pharaoh's army. Moses, however, calmly ordered, "Stand firm and see the salvation of God!" Suddenly a powerful east wind began to blow, clearing a path of dry ground at the bottom of the sea. Walled-up water stood at attention, forming a channel through which Israel could pass.

At that moment, each Israelite made a choice through an act of faith to cast his own life into the hands of the God who had parted the waters. All the Israelites walked down the western shore of the Red Sea believing that they would arrive alive on the eastern shore. Paul later characterized this act of faith as a baptism unto Moses, an immersion that came to be characterized as a death, burial, and resurrection to a different legal status. Just as later proselytes were legally changed from strangers to Israelites when they came up out of the waters of the *mikveh* (baptism), so when the Israelites passed through the Red Sea, they emerged on the other side with a change of status, no longer slaves but free men.

What was to be fulfilled in this new nation of believers in the God of creation would ever be founded upon that one eventful night in Egypt when God provided the lamb as a vicarious and efficacious atonement, a means of escape that secured their freedom. And, to ensure that each generation would not forget what God had done, the Lord decreed that every Israelite home would forever celebrate the Passover each year by eating the roasted lamb, the bitter herbs, and the unleavened bread. Every Israelite was instructed to celebrate the Passover as an anamnesis, a virtual reenactment of the original event wherein one could relive the Passover in a very personal way. The first of the year for Israel would be not just the spring when everything is renewed; it would be the time of redemption, the time of freedom.

A SECOND PASSOVER, A REFORMED FAITH

For fifteen centuries, the Israelites had faithfully fulfilled God's commandment, celebrating the Passover each year with their families and friends. In one such celebration, a group of Torah-observant Jews gathered around their Rabbi in a rented upper-level banquet room. "I have desired to celebrate this Passover with you before I suffer," he had declared (Luke 22:15). Systematically, he and his disciples followed the *seder* of observance that the sages of previous generations had prescribed. They ate the roasted lamb, dipped their bread in the bitter herbs (John 13:26), and sang the *Hallel* Psalms (Matthew 26:30).

This was the scene on the eve of Passover when *Yeshua HaMashiach* shared his last Passover celebration with his twelve disciples. During this Passover, however, Jesus instituted a New Covenant Passover celebration that would forever be a memorial to demonstrate the Lord's death until his return. "Take, eat; this is my body," he declared of the unleavened bread. "Drink ye all of it; this is the new covenant in my blood," he said of the Passover wine. For the first time, they celebrated the momentous deliverance that was to occur on the very next day when the Lord was to consummate his role as "the Lamb of God who takes away the sins of the world," as John the Baptizer had described him three years earlier (John 1:29).

At the conclusion of the *seder*, these Passover celebrants went out to the Mount of Olives. There Jesus prayed for hours in the Garden of Gethsemane near the Kidron Valley. All that was human in him cried out to his Father for release from the bitter cup of suffering that he was to endure the following day. Finally, however, he uttered those immortal words of submission, "Not my will but thine be done." Just then, his betraying disciple, leading a band of men from the high priest, kissed him on the cheek, delivering him into the hands of his enemies.

During that night and early the following morning, Jesus was taken before various civil and religious authorities, none of whom could find fault in him. Just as the Passover lamb was to be "without blemish" (Exodus 12:5), so Jesus "offered himself without blemish to God" (Hebrews 9:14) so that all who would believe in him would be purified and presented "without blemish before the presence of his glory with rejoicing" (Jude 1:24). Despite his lack of guilt, the political conspiracy between the Roman civil authorities and some of the aristocratic, apostate religious leaders condemned Jesus to death. He was led outside the city of Jerusalem to a spot called the Place of the Skull, Golgotha, where he was nailed to the cross he had carried, crucified for all to see, the Son of God suspended between heaven and earth, the Lamb of God bleeding and dying for the sins of the world.

On this momentous Passover, at the moment when the Son of God declared, "It is finished," and surrendered his last breath, the massive curtain of the temple was torn from the top to the bottom by the hand of God, creating a new and open means of access to God for all men. The means of atonement had been made. Again, God declared, "When I see the blood, I will pass over you." All men could now come boldly before the throne of God, bearing the blood of the Passover Lamb, the Messiah himself. This freedom was of far greater consequence than that at the Red Sea: this was a freedom from the bondage of sin that brought abundant life and the promise of eternal life.

Again, as it was in Egypt, it was some time before the final liberation was achieved. The sacrifice of the lamb secured the downpayment on freedom, but the Red Sea crossing was required for the total liberty that was fully realized when Israel came to Sinai and entered into a covenant to become God's nation of priests. Likewise, the price for eternal freedom was paid as the blood of the Lamb spilled from the cross on Golgotha's hill; however, it was three days later when the Son of God came forth from his entombment, triumphant over death, hell, and the grave, having crossed over the chasm between the dead and the living and ascended into the presence of God in heaven. The death, burial, and resurrection that was prefigured in Israel's Red Sea immersion forever provided the way to freedom from sin and access to eternal life for all who would believe and apply the Lamb's blood to the doorposts and lintels of their hearts.

Though some had been resurrected from the grave by words of faith from prophets, never had one risen of his own accord. "I have the power to lay my life down and to take it up again," Jesus had said, for "I am the resurrection and the life." When the massive stone was rolled away and Jesus came forth, he demonstrated his power over sin and death. He fully conquered in his own life the last enemy that will finally be subdued for all men at the end of the age. The miracle of Passover had just taken on new and more profound proportions for the Jewish disciples of the Savior. They were commissioned to share the good news of God's new Passover provision with the entire world, making disciples of all nations.

For those earliest Christians, Passover observance each year took on new meaning. As it had always been for them, it continued to be a celebration of God's deliverance from Egyptian bondage. As Jews, they were required by the terms of their covenant to remember the Passover; however, it now took on even more profound significance, for it also became a time for celebrating the finished work of Calvary, the death of the spotless Lamb who brought freedom from sin and the gift of eternal life.

Even when these earliest Christians followed their Lord's command and took the good news to the Gentiles, these new initiates into the faith of Jesus were instructed to observe the Passover. The apostle officially designated as the church's ambassador to the Gentiles, Rabbi Paul, a student of Gamliel, gave this recommendation: "Because Christ our Passover is sacrificed for us, therefore let us observe the festival . . . with the unleavened bread of sincerity and truth" (1 Corinthians 5:8). He continued to underscore the new covenant observance for Passover: "For I received from the Lord that which I also delivered to you: that the Lord Jesus on the same night in which he was betrayed took bread; and when he had given thanks, he broke it and said, 'Take, eat; this is my body which is broken for you; do this in remembrance of me.' In the same manner he also took the cup after supper, saying, 'This cup is the new covenant in my blood. This do, as often as you drink it, in remembrance of me.' For as often as you eat this bread and drink this cup, you proclaim the Lord's death till he comes" (1 Corinthians 11:23-26). Indeed, references to "eating the flesh and drinking the blood" of Jesus (John 6:53) can be understood only in the context of the Passover.

For the Christian believers, the unleavened bread of the Passover spoke of their liberation from sin and false teaching, including the "leaven" of much of the contemporary religious establishment, which included greed (Matthew 23:14), intolerance (Matthew 23:29-33), ostentatious hypocrisy (Matthew 23:25-28), misdirected fervor (Matthew 23:15), and skepticism (Matthew 22:23ff). The paradigm is clear in Hebrew where *chametz* (leaven) means "bitterness," the result of sin and unethical conduct, while *matzah* (unleavened bread) means "sweet without sourness," the result of tasting and seeing that the Lord is good and ingesting his Word which is sweeter than honey. Believers in the Messiah had left the life of bitterness, enslaved to sin and evil concepts, and had embraced a life of consuming all the Lamb of God (as their ancestors had eaten all of the *paschal* lamb), conforming themselves to the image of God's dear Son.

APOSTOLIC OBSERVANCE

When the time came for the first Passover following Jesus' ascension, the growing band of Jewish believers assembled in their homes to fulfill the commandment regarding remembrance of the Passover. This time, however, they added the order which Jesus had commissioned to the traditional *seder* that the sages had outlined for Passover observance. They remembered two Passovers, one which secured their freedom from Egyptian bondage and the other which liberated them from sin through the shed blood of the Passover Lamb himself.

This order continued unbroken in all the Jewish households of the Christian church. Then, when the church opened the doors of faith to the Gentile nations on the basis of simple faith in the atonement of Jesus, its Jewish leaders continued their observance of the Torah as it had been expanded and completed by the teaching and example of Jesus, the Messiah. Their expanded and renewed faith represented a reformation of restoration (Hebrews 9:10), a return to the Torah's original intent of inculcating a life of lovingkindness rather than the superficial punctilious observance of commandments that characterized many in their day. A prominent feature of this reformed faith was the annual observance of Passover, again celebrating two deliverances: the Exodus and Calvary.

A CONTINUING HISTORY OF OBSERVANCE

The celebration of Passover (on the fourteenth day of the month Nisan according to the Jewish calendar) continued in the early church for more than three centuries. The Ethiopic version of the Epistle of the Apostles (circa 150 A.D.), declares, "And you therefore celebrate the remembrance of my death [the Passover]; then will one of you . . . be thrown into prison, and he will be grieved and sorrowful, for while you celebrate the Passover he who is in custody did not celebrate it with you." Apollinaris, bishop of Hierapolis (circa 170 A.D.), declared unequivocally: "The fourteenth of Nisan is the true Passover of the Lord, the great Sacrifice; instead of the lamb we have the Son of God . . . who was buried on the day of the Passover."

As the church became increasingly Gentile in leadership and demographics, a gradual shift away from what by then were considered "Jewish" practices developed. For the Western Church, this replacement of the Jewish foundations of the Christian faith reached a point of culmination in the time of the Roman Emperor

Constantine. During the Council of Nicea in 325 A.D., Constantine demanded that the church no longer have anything in common with the Jews whom he viewed as the "parricides of our Lord." With his insistence, church leaders changed the time of celebration from Nisan 14 on the Jewish calendar to the first Sunday after the vernal equinox on the Julian calendar. This celebration eventually came to be known in English as Easter, named after the Saxon goddess of spring and light, *Eastre*, in honor of whom a festival was celebrated in April.

Even after the practice of Passover observance had been discarded by the Western Church, Epiphanius (circa 315-403 A.D.) continued to report the fact that earlier church leaders had insisted that Passover be observed each year on Nisan 14, saying, "You shall not change the calculation of the time, but you shall celebrate it at the same time as your brethren who came out from the circumcision. With them observe the Passover."

The Eastern (Orthodox) Church continued to observe Passover on Nisan 14 until the eleventh century. Various Christians through the centuries have remained faithful to the idea of remembering the death of Jesus on the day on which he gave his life for man's salvation: the day of Passover.

FOUNDATIONAL EVENTS

Passover, then, the fourteenth day of Nisan, the first month of the Jewish calendar, has forever established itself as foundational both to Judaism and to Christianity. In both cases, it speaks of freedom and liberation from oppression. In both cases, it speaks of God's forgiveness because of acts of faith on the part of his people that provided the means by which the demands for divine justice are met so that he can pass over. And, because of the momentous events of this day, both Jews and Christians are called to remember God's mighty acts and to celebrate his goodness throughout all their generations even to the end of the age when the Messiah will once again commemorate the Lord's Passover in his kingdom.

Preparations for a Passover Seder

The following elements should be prepared in advance of the Passover Seder celebration:

For the Leader:
Candlesticks and white candles, two if Passover is on a Sabbath, otherwise one for each participant.
One bowl of saltwater.
One shankbone of a lamb (or any roasted bone of a levitically permitted animal, symbolizing the Passover lamb), roasted until brown.
Three entire pieces of *matzah* inserted either in a *matzah* bag or between four linen napkins.
One roasted egg, first boiled and then roasted in a frying pan until brown.
One bowl of water with a towel.
Four ornate cups, goblets, or wine glasses.
Wine or grape juice.

For the Celebrants:
Place settings for each, including plates and silverware (can be paper and plastic).
Parsley–two sprigs per person.
Bitter Herbs–usually ½ teaspoon per person. Fresh horseradish is preferred.
Charoset–at least 1 tablespoon per person. Chop apples and nuts; mix them with honey, cinnamon, and wine or grape juice.
Saltwater–one small bowl of intensely salty water well-mixed (kosher salt is best) for each 4-5 people.
Matzah–enough for each person to have approximately one-fourth of a full piece of *matzah*.
One cup per person.
Wine or grape juice adequate to fill each celebrant's cup about one-third full four times.

A Christian Celebration for
Passover
(A CHRISTIAN HAGGADAH)

INTRODUCTION

Leader:

We are honored and grateful that we have been invited by the Eternal God of heaven and earth to celebrate the Passover that he so graciously has provided for us as families among his chosen people. Our spiritual forebears were slaves in Egypt when God Almighty with his outstretched arm delivered them and us from bondage on this very night and brought all of us unto himself to redeem us and make us a kingdom of priests. We were also slaves to sin when the Eternal Father on this very day gave the gift of his only begotten Son, Jesus Christ (*Yeshua HaMashiach*), to adopt us as his children and to deliver us from the power of the evil one.

We come to this table not necessarily because our linear ancestors were delivered from Egypt but because we have become naturalized citizens in the commonwealth of Israel through our faith in Jesus Christ, the one who brought Israel's light to the nations. Whether native born or naturalized, we are all fellow citizens in God's nation and among his chosen people, Israel.

Because the God of Abraham, Isaac, and Jacob has instructed his children to keep the Passover throughout all generations and because Jesus, our Passover, has been sacrificed for us, as a part of the nation of Israel,

Leader and People:
   Therefore, let us observe the festival with the unleavened bread of sincerity and truth.

THE HAGADDAH

Leader:
   Passover is the oldest and most important of the biblical festivals. It is foundational to God's people in that on this very day the miraculous event occurred that liberated the children of Israel from slavery and brought them to the mountain of God where they corporately joined with the Eternal to be his chosen people. Passover is also foundational to Christianity in that on this very day Jesus the Christ (*Yeshua HaMashiach*) bore in his body on the cross of Calvary the sins of the entire world and provided the eternal sacrifice by which men of all nations are reconciled to God.
   Because believers in God are commanded by him to "remember that you were slaves in Egypt," observant Jews consider that not only their ancestors, but also they themselves were enslaved in Pharaoh's onerous bondage and that they personally were delivered by the outstretched arm of God. This is the reason that the observance of Passover has been commanded by the Creator "for ever, throughout all your generations," and this is the reason we, as part of the Israel of God, observe it today.
   Israel had been enslaved for over 200 years, forced into ever more difficult and torturous labor to build the splendor of Egyptian monuments. The bondage grew more severe and the task-masters more harsh until finally the Israelites cried out to God for deliverance. God's response was to send a deliverer. Moses, an Israelite who had been reared as the son of Pharaoh's daughter, came face to face with God's voice that issued from a burning bush, saying, "Tell Pharaoh, 'Let my people go.'"
   With the help of his brother Aaron, Moses delivered this fateful message to the world's most powerful ruler. The results were predictable, for even human history's greatest diplomat could not have easily secured the Israelites' release. Ten plagues were poured out upon Egypt. Each plague grew in intensity until finally, the last

of the ten plagues was pronounced upon Egypt: all the firstborn of Egypt were to die as God himself passed through the land in one night of terror.

As the night of Passover approached, all Israelite families were instructed to sacrifice an unblemished lamb at the threshold of their houses' door. Then, the blood at the threshold was applied with a bunch of hyssop to the doorposts and lintel of the house. God had said, "When I see the blood, I will pass over you." The blood encircling the doors of their houses was a public demonstration of each Israelite family's confidence in God and his word.

As God passed through Egypt, all the houses where blood was not applied suffered the loss of their firstborn. When Pharaoh realized that his obstinacy had resulted in the widespread loss of life in Egypt, he relented and ordered the Israelites to leave Egypt, giving them whatever they needed.

The miraculous events of the Passover season were of such magnitude that all of Israel was commanded to remember God's deliverance "throughout all your generations." Each generation was to remember that they were there, enduring the slavery, fearfully offering the paschal lamb, faithfully applying the blood to the door, triumphantly departing from Egypt, standing in trepidation at the Red Sea, marching confidently through the divided waters, watching in awe the destruction of Egypt's armies, and singing the song of triumph.

People:
We, too, were there!

Leader:
Some fifteen hundred years later, as the vast majority of the world languished in bondage to sin, God expanded his covenant with Israel to include all men. The nations that had not known God were to be brought near to him and included within his chosen people by the provision of a perfect and eternally efficacious sacrifice for sin. God determined that his only begotten Son, Jesus Christ (*Yeshua HaMashiach*), would enter into the world when Mary, a virgin daughter of Israel, was overshadowed by the Holy Spirit and conceived the Son of Man. The entire world was to be saved as a Son of Israel, was to take Israel's light to the nations.

Jesus became the doorway to eternal life in much the same manner as the doors of Israelite households were prepared at the time of the exodus. With five wounds (his head, his back, his hands, his feet, and his side), Jesus' entire body was encircled with blood. As the Paschal Lamb, he provided the blood by which God passed over the sins of mankind, and he became the door to eternal life.

In anguish he was nailed to the cross. Six excruciating hours later, he exclaimed, "It is finished," and he died. At that moment, the massive curtain in the temple was torn from the top to the bottom, as God created a new access into the heavenly Holy of Holies. As thousands of his Jewish brethren were offering their family Passover lambs in the temple, the Eternal Father in Heaven was offering the Lamb of God who came to take away the sins of the world on the cross of Calvary, Golgotha, the "Place of the Skull."

But the story only begins there, for three days later he arose and ascended into Glory, to be seated at his Father's right hand, interceding for all the human race. Since that time, all men everywhere have been welcomed to the foot of the cross to be reconciled to God through the atonement of the Passover Lamb. Every knee that has bowed in repentance and contrition has been raised again in the newness of life with the promise of a resurrection into life eternal. In a very real sense, therefore, all who have accepted Jesus as Lord and Savior can say:

Leader and People:
    We, too, were there!
Leader:
    The struggle for freedom is continuous. In every age there are new elements that strive for mastery over the human spirit, enslaving man anew by binding them either to the desires of our flesh or to human systems. Each generation is obligated to continue the dynamic march toward freedom. The Hebrew word translated "freedom" is dynamic, not static. This is to say that "freedom" is an action, not a state of being. Our freedom in Christ likewise is not simply a state of being but a maximal dynamic, an ongoing series of liberating events manifest continually in our lives.
Leader:
    We, therefore, see ourselves as full participants in the liberation of the Exodus as well as the liberty of Calvary, wherein Jesus' self-

sacrifice as our Passover Lamb has made us free. We dedicate our lives to the struggle of freedom for all humankind.

THE SEDER

Leader:

The sages of Israel have provided a *seder*, an "order" which ensures that the Passover meal is properly and worthily observed. A generation before the time of Jesus, Hillel explained that only three elements were necessary for the proper observance of Passover: the lamb, unleavened bread, and bitter herbs. Other sages, however, added elements to the *Haggadah* (narrative) in its proper order.

Leader and People:

We join our hearts in celebrating this joyous festival, the Lord's Passover.

CHECKING FOR LEAVEN

(Though this exercise is not required at the seder, *families and congregations may consider it profitable. If so, the leader will have hidden ten pieces of leavened bread in the home or sanctuary prior to the* seder.*)*

Leader:

God's "Divine Instruction, the Torah, commanded Israel to remove all leaven from their houses.

Men:

"Seven days shall you eat unleavened bread; on the first day you shall remove leaven from your houses" (Exodus 12:15).

Leader:

The Apostolic Writings agree that we must remove the leaven of sin from our lives.

Women:

"Purge out therefore the old leaven, that you may be a new lump, since you are truly unleavened" (1 Corinthians 5:7).

Leader:

Because of God's commandment that all leaven be removed from every household prior to the Passover, extensive and thorough efforts are made in every observant Jewish home to clean the entire house, particularly areas for preparing and eating food. The Western world has received this tradition as "spring cleaning."

After the house is thoroughly cleaned so that all leaven is removed, a parent (or head of household) intentionally hides ten pieces of leavened bread (*chametz*) in the house in order to reinforce this object lesson to the children. Then, the children are invited to search for the leaven. Upon discovering it, however, they are not permitted to touch it. Instead, the parent uses a feather and a wooden spoon and gently and thoroughly removes the leaven (usually to be burned the following day).

This is a great object lesson for us as children of our heavenly Father. In Jewish tradition, leaven came to represent the potential for corruption and sin. In Christian tradition, leaven represents sin and unfaithfulness to the Word and will of God. We are invited by our Father to search for even the hidden sins in our lives; however, when we discover them, we cannot deal with them ourselves. We must turn to our Father who gently and thoroughly removes them from our lives and casts them into the fire.

Leader:

Now, children, can you find the ten pieces of leaven?

(When the bread is found, the leader uses the feather and wooden spoon to collect it. It may be deposited outside the home or sanctuary.)

Leader:

The Apostolic Writings instruct us to observe the Lord's Passover worthily and in a proper manner, first by examining ourselves to see if we are in the faith. "For if we would judge ourselves," we are told, "we would not be judged" (1 Corinthians 11:31).

With David of old, we cry out to our Creator:

Leader and People:

"Cleanse me from secret faults. . . . Purge me with hyssop, and I shall be clean; wash me, and I shall be whiter than snow" (Psalm 19:12; 51:7).

Leader:

Our advocate with the Father, Jesus Christ the righteous, is faithful to cleanse us from all our sins. "Blessed is he whose transgression is forgiven, whose sin is covered" (Romans 4:7).

Leader and People:

We receive your pardon, O Father, and we rejoice in our fellowship with you through *Ruach haKodesh*, the "Holy Spirit."

LIGHTING OF THE PASSOVER CANDLES

Leader:

Our *seder* begins with the lighting of the Passover candles, an honor that goes to the mother of the home. As God honored Mary to bring the Light of God into the world, so he honors the woman to kindle the festival lights. Light has always symbolized the Divine Presence manifest in ancient times in the *Shekhinah* and in the New Covenant in *Ruach haKodesh* whose seven lamps of fire burn before the throne of God as well as in our hearts. "The people who sat in darkness have seen a great light; and upon those who sat in the region and shadow of death light has dawned" (Matthew 4:16), for " . . . a virgin shall conceive, and bear a son, and shall call his name Immanuel [God with us]" (Isaiah 7:14).

Mother or Female Leader:

We are gathered with loved ones and friends for this joyous celebration of our Lord's Passover. What we demonstrate is our fulfillment of our Lord's instruction:

People:

"You shall keep the feast of Unleavened Bread, for on this very day I brought your hosts out of the land of Egypt: therefore you shall observe this day, throughout the generations, as an ordinance for ever" (Exodus 12:17).

Mother or Female Leader:

Blessed are you, O Lord our God, King of the universe, who has preserved our lives so that we may celebrate your festival. As we kindle these festival lights, may the light of your presence overshadow us so that we may discern the significance of this celebration.

(The mother/female leader lights the Passover candles. In a corporate setting, one woman may light candles at each table.)

THE FIRST CUP
THE CUP OF SANCTIFICATION

(The leader will have four ornate cups, wine glasses, or goblets to demonstrate the four cups of Passover; however, individual participants will have only one cup that is partially filled four times preferably with red wine [or grape juice].)

Leader:

The Passover story (*Haggadah*) centers on the express fourfold promise of God to Israel. We fill our cups four times to celebrate God's full and free deliverance that brought us out of Egypt. Herein we remember our Father's words:

People:

"I am the Lord; [1] I will bring you out from under the burdens of the Egyptians [*Sanctification*], [2] I will rescue you from their bondage [*Deliverance and Judgment*], and [3] I will redeem you with an outstretched arm and with great judgments [*Redemption*]. [4] I will take you as my people, and I will be your God [*Thanksgiving and Consummation*]" (Exodus 6:6-7).

(Both the leader and the people's cups are partially filled.)

Leader: *(as everyone elevates the cup)*

בָּרוּךְ אַתָּה יְיָ אֱלֹהֵינוּ מֶלֶךְ הָעוֹלָם בּוֹרֵא פְּרִי הַגָּפֶן:

BARUKH ATAH ADONAI, ELOHEYNU, MELEKH HA'OLAM, BOREY PRI HAGAFEN.

Blessed are you, O Lord our God, King of the universe, who has created the fruit of the vine.

Leader and People:

Blessed are you, O Lord our God, King of the universe, who has chosen us from among all people, and exalted us above all languages and has sanctified us with your commandments, and with love have you given us, O Lord, our God, solemn days for joy, festivals and seasons for gladness: this day of the feast of Unleavened Bread, the season of our freedom: a holy convocation, a memorial of the departure from Egypt: for you have chosen us, and sanctified us above all people: and you have caused us to inherit your holy festivals with joy and gladness. Blessed are you, O Lord, who sanctifies Israel and the seasons.

Blessed are you, O Lord our God, King of the universe, who has preserved us alive, sustained us, and brought us to enjoy this season.

Leader:

We praise you because you fulfill your promises to all your children. Whenever evil ones oppress us, your outstretched hand delivers us and brings us freedom, and we are restored. When the Evil One held us in the clutches of our own sin, you made provision for us through the shedding of the blood of your Son that we could be free, free from sin and inheritors of eternal life.

People:

"I am the LORD: I will bring you out from under the burden of the Egyptians" (Exodus 6:6). "Take this, and divide it among yourselves: for I say unto you, I will not drink of the fruit of the vine, until the kingdom of God shall come" (Luke 22:17-18); "Therefore if the Son makes you free, you shall be free indeed . . . Sanctify them by your truth, your word is truth . . . and you shall know the truth, and the truth shall make you free" (John 8:36, 32).

(All drink of the first cup, the Cup of Sanctification and Freedom.)

GREEN VEGETABLE

Leader:

As a part of this Passover we eat of a green vegetable dipped in salt water. Partaking of the salt water reminds us of the tears that the Israelites shed as slaves in Egypt. It also helps us remember that the way of the transgressor is bitter and that our sins bring us great sorrow and pain. We also recall the salty water of the Red Sea. Then, we vividly remember the bitter tears that our Lord Jesus shed in the Garden of Gethsemane when he considered the agonizing suffering and the awesome task of assuming to himself the sins of us all. We also recall that during his lonely ordeal of submission to the will of his Father, his sweat became as drops of blood.

Jesus was the *Logos* "enfleshed," who came to bring abundant life to all. For this reason we eat a fresh, green spring vegetable to give us a vivid image of the life that liberates us from slavery, the life that gives us freedom from sin, and the eternal life that is the promise to all the righteous in the resurrection. By our acceptance of Jesus as Messiah and Lord, we have experienced the newness of life (Romans 6:4).

People:

"If anyone is in Christ, he is a new creation . . . If the Spirit of him who raised Jesus from the dead dwells in you, he who raised Christ from the dead will also give life to your mortal bodies through his Spirit who dwells in you" (2 Corinthians 5:17; Romans 8:11).

Leader (taking a piece of parsley or lettuce and lifting it up):

בָּרוּךְ אַתָּה יְיָ אֱלֹהֵינוּ מֶלֶךְ הָעוֹלָם בּוֹרֵא פְּרִי הָאֲדָמָה:

BARUKH ATAH ADONAI ELOHEYNU, MELEKH HA'OLAM, BOREY PRI HA'ADAMAH.

Blessed are You, O Lord our God, King of the universe, who creates the fruit of the earth.

(All dip the piece of parsley in salt water and eat it.)

BREAKING OF UNLEAVENED BREAD

Leader:

In our *seder* we have specially prepared unleavened bread called *matzah*. The Hebrew term for unleavened bread, *matzah*, means "sweet" and is contrasted with the Hebrew word for leavened bread, *chametz*, which means "bitter."

People:

"O taste and see that the Lord is good" (Psalm 34:8). "How sweet are your words to my taste, sweeter than honey to my mouth!" (Psalm 119:103).

Leader:

You will notice that in the process of baking this *matzah*, it was pierced in order to ensure that it did not rise from incipient yeast. In the baking process brown stripes are created along these pierced rows. This brings vividly to our minds the suffering of our Messiah.

People:

"He was wounded for our transgressions, he was bruised for our iniquities . . . and by his stripes we are healed" (Isaiah 53:5); ". . . they pierced my hands and my feet" (Psalm 22:16); ". . . they shall look on me whom they have pierced . . ." (Zechariah 12:10).

Leader:

The sages have prescribed that the unleavened bread, one of the three essential elements of the Passover *seder*, be received from three pieces of *matzah* separated in the folds of a napkin or in the three compartments of a specially designed bag. The three pieces of *matzah*, called by the sages "Unity," represent Abraham, Isaac, and Jacob as well as the three divisions of the Hebrew Scriptures: *Torah* (Law), *Nevi'im* (Prophets), and *Ketuvim* (Writings). They also represent the three levels of divine service in Israel:

the Priests, the Levites, and the people of Israel.

It is also said that the three pieces of *matzah* can be traced to the three measures of flour which Abraham asked Sarah to bake when the angels visited him, according to tradition, on the eve of Passover. Abraham's instruction to Sarah to "be quick" in taking three measures of flour and making cakes parallels God's instruction on Passover that the Israelites eat the *matzah* in haste.

Many early Jewish Christians celebrated the Passover with three pieces of *matzah* to represent the three elements of the one God: Father, Son, and Holy Spirit. Furthermore, it is the middle of the three pieces of *matzah* that is broken into two pieces, symbolizing the human body of Jesus that was broken for sin.

All *matzah* on *Pesach* is called *Lechem Oni*, "the Bread of Affliction." It was the bread that the Israelites ate at the time of their greatest suffering in Egypt. It also symbolizes the broken body of Jesus who was afflicted when the Father placed upon him the sins of us all.

People:

"I am the living bread which came down from heaven. If anyone eats of this bread, he will live for ever" (John 6:51). "For indeed Christ our Passover was sacrificed for us" (1 Corinthians 5:7).

Leader:

In the *seder*, half of the middle *matzah* is wrapped in a linen napkin and hidden from view, later to be discovered by the children and redeemed. Traditionally this part of the middle *matzah* is called the *afikomin*, derived from the Greek *apókomein*, meaning "off-cut," the choice part of meat that was cut off before the Greek banquet began and was reserved to be eaten as "dessert."

People:

"For he was cut off from the land of the living; for the transgressions of my people he was stricken" (Isaiah 53:8); however, he was discovered to be alive, resurrected in a glorious body (Philippians 3:21).

Leader:

After we hide the *afikomin*, the remaining half of the middle *matzah* is returned to its place between the two whole *matzot*.

THE FOUR QUESTIONS

Leader:

The Word of God tells us that our children will ask questions. God has instructed us to tell them the story of the Passover so that they may know the Lord for themselves. It is both a sacred duty and a privilege to rehearse the miraculous acts of God in the story of Passover.

(The youngest child present, or different children, should ask these four questions. The most senior person present should answer the questions.)

Child:

"Why is this night different from all other nights?"

Elder:

The Israelites were slaves to Pharaoh in Egypt when the Lord redeemed them with a mighty hand. If the Lord had not taken them out of Egypt, their children and grandchildren would still be slaves in Egypt. This is why it is our duty to tell the story of our Exodus from Egypt. The more one tells this story, the more praiseworthy he is.

Child:

On all other nights we eat leavened and unleavened bread; on this night only unleavened bread?

Elder:

Because the Israelites left Egypt in haste, they did not have time for their bread to rise before they had to bake it; therefore, they ate only unleavened bread. Just as the Israelites left leaven behind them in Egypt, we also leave the sin of our old lives behind us when we enter the new life of faith in Jesus our Messiah.

Child:

On all other nights we eat any kind of vegetable; on this night only bitter herbs?

Elder:

Eating bitter herbs helps us remember that the Israelites endured much bitterness and pain in Egypt's slavery. It also causes us to recall the suffering that Jesus endured on the cross.

Child:

On all other nights we are not required to dip in salt even once; on this night we dip twice?

Elder:

Dipping in salt water causes us to remember the tears shed by the Israelites in Egypt. It also helps us recall the agony that Jesus suffered in Gethsemane as he faced the suffering on the cross. We dip once to remember the slavery of Egypt, and we dip the second time to feel the pain of the price that Jesus paid to release us from bondage to sin.

Leader:

Narrating the Exodus story fulfills the commandment that we are to tell our children what occurred in that fateful time in Egypt.

People:

"And you shall tell your son in that day, saying, 'This is done because of what the Lord did unto me when I came forth out of Egypt' " (Exodus 13:8).

Leader (*lifting the* seder *plate with his right hand and the* matzah *with his left hand):*

This is the bread of affliction which the Israelites ate in the land of Egypt; let all that are hungry enter and eat; and all who are in want, come and celebrate the Passover. This year we celebrate it here, but next year we hope to celebrate it in the land of Israel.

Leader:

Our Lord Jesus himself said, "The bread of God is he who comes down from heaven and gives life to the world . . . I am the bread of life. He who comes to me shall never hunger. . ." (John 6:33, 35).

Leader:

This year we celebrate the Passover as slaves to our humanity; next year as free, resurrected men we eat it anew at the Messiah's table in the Kingdom of God!

People:

"I will not drink of this fruit of the vine from now on until that day when I drink it anew with you in my Father's kingdom" (Matthew 26:29); "Blessed are those who are called to the marriage supper of the Lamb" (Revelation 19:9).

REHEARSING THE EXODUS STORY

Leader:

Once our spiritual ancestors were slaves to Pharaoh in Eygpt, but the Lord in his mercy through the Passover brought them out of that land with a mighty hand and an outstretched arm.

People:

Had God not rescued them from the hand of the destroyer, surely we and our children and our children's children would still be enslaved, deprived of freedom and dignity.

Leader:

Once we worshipped idols and were enslaved by our sins, but God in his goodness and mercy through Jesus, the Passover Lamb, forgave our transgressions and called us to be his people.

People:

Therefore, tonight is different from other nights because we have gathered to remember both God's deliverance from slavery and his deliverance from sin. We remember who we are and what God has done for us, and we rehearse for our children the story of God's deliverance at both the first Passover and at the New Covenant Passover.

Leader:

The Eternal God of heaven promised Abraham and Sarah that they would produce a great people through whom all the nations of the earth would be blessed. This promise was renewed to Isaac and again to Jacob. When the sovereignty of God made provision for preserving the household of Jacob by saving also the nation of Egypt, Joseph was delivered into Egypt and tried by the Word of the Lord. He became prime minister in Egypt and devised a plan to sustain all the people from seven years of famine. For this, he and his family were greatly honored.

Later a Pharaoh arose "who knew not Joseph," and enslaved the Israelites, imposing upon them backbreaking labor. He even ordered every newborn Israelite boy drowned in the River Nile. The Israelites knew nothing but labor, suffering, and tears.

People:

Our fathers cried out to God seeking an end to Egyptian oppression. God heard their cry and raised up Moses through miraculous intervention and in time brought him before Pharaoh to make the divine declaration: "Let my people go."

Leader:

Pharaoh's heart was hardened. He refused the divine imperative and only increased the suffering of our fathers. The Eternal God sent ten plagues upon Egypt so that Pharaoh might know the divine power and submit to the divine directive.

It was God himself who delivered them: "On that same night I will pass through Egypt . . ."

People:

I, and not an angel.

Leader:

". . . and strike down every firstborn, both men and animals."

People:

I, and not a seraph.

Leader:

". . . and I will bring judgment on all the gods of Egypt. . ."

People:

I, and not a messenger.

Leader:

". . . I am the LORD." (Exodus 12:12)

People:

I myself and none other.

THE TEN PLAGUES AND THE CUP OF DELIVERANCE AND JUDGMENT

(The second of four cups in now poured. Pour only a small amount, since no one will drink of this cup.)

Leader:

We now come to the time for recognizing the second cup, the Cup of Deliverance. This cup is one of joy; however, it is diminished by the fact that the Egyptians, who are also God's children, suffered because of Pharaoh's evil heart. The lives of those Egyptians were sacrificed to effect God's will. Now, as we recount the ten plagues, we spill a drop of wine from our cups for each plague to remember the judgment that comes upon men for worshipping false gods and bringing evil into the world.

(As each plague is named, everyone uses a finger to take a drop of wine from the cup and let it drip onto a plate, symbolizing the finger of God's judgment for sin.)*

Leader:	**People:**
Dam	Blood
Leader:	**People:**
Tzfardeia	Frogs
Leader:	**People:**
Kinim	Vermin
Leader:	**People:**
Arov	Swarming Creatures
Leader:	**People:**
Dever	Pestilence
Leader:	**People:**
Sh'chin	Boils
Leader:	**People:**
Barad	Hail
Leader:	**People:**
Arbeh	Locusts
Leader:	**People:**
Choshech	Darkness
Leader:	**People:**
Makat B'Chorot	Slaying the First-Born

Leader:

Reeling from the effects of the final plague, Pharaoh relented and ordered the Israelites to leave Egypt. Again, Israel had been spared from the effects of this final plague by God's plan called "The Passover." The blood of a Passover lamb was applied to the doorposts and lintels of all Israelite homes so that when God passed through Egypt requiring the lives of all firstborn, he could "pass over" the houses where he saw the blood.

*Each of the ten plagues demonstrated God's judgment upon one of the Egyptian gods: 1) Blood: *Osiris*, god of the Nile River; 2) Frogs: *Hekt*, frog-headed goddess; 3) Lice: *Seb*, earth god (the dust was turned into lice); 4) Swarming Creatures: *Scarabus*, the worshipped dung beetle; 5) Dying Cattle: *Apis*, the bull god; 6) Boils: *Neit*, god of health; 7) Hail: *Shu*, god of the atmosphere; 8) Locusts: *Serapia*, god of the locusts; 9) Darkness: *Ra*, sun god; 10) Death of Firstborn: the incarnate deities, Pharaoh and his son.

People:

Thanks be to God for the provision of the Passover lamb that saved Israel from the final plague. Thanks be to God for providing the Passover Lamb, *Yeshua HaMashiach*, who takes away the sins of the world and saves us from the final second death.

Leader:

With this cup we celebrate God's deliverance that also brought judgment upon his enemies. God has delivered us from bondage to freedom, from darkness to light, from sorrow to joy.

People:

We rejoice, therefore, and praise him for his boundless grace.

(The second cup is poured out without drinking.)

THE THREE ESSENTIAL ELEMENTS

Leader:

Rabbi Gamliel, disciple of Hillel and teacher of Paul, insisted that "whoever does not discuss the following three things at the Passover festival has not fulfilled his duty, namely: *Pesach*, *Matzah*, and *Maror*."

Our Lord Jesus also partook of these three essentials on the night of the last supper before his death. "[Jesus] said unto them, 'With fervent desire I have desired to eat this Passover [the *Pesach* lamb] with you before I suffer.' " (Luke 22:15); "And he took bread [*matzah*], gave thanks and broke it, and gave it to them, saying, 'This is my body which is given for you; do this in remembrance of me.' " (Luke 22:19); "Jesus answered, 'It is he to whom I will give a piece of bread when I have dipped it [in the *maror*].' " (John 13:26).

Leader *(removing the shankbone from the* seder *plate and holding it up):*

The Passover sacrifice that the Israelites ate while the temple was standing signified the offering by which the Holy One passed over their houses in Egypt, as it is written:

People:

"You shall say, 'It is the Passover sacrifice of the LORD, who passed over the houses of the children of Israel in Egypt, when he struck the Egyptians, and delivered our households.'

" (Exodus 12:27). ". . . every man shall take for himself . . . a lamb for a household . . . your lamb shall be without blemish, a male of the first year . . . ye shall keep it up until the fourteenth day of the same month. Then the whole assembly of the congregation of Israel shall kill it at twilight. And they shall take of some of the blood and put it on the two doorposts and on the lintel of the houses where they shall eat it. . . . And thus you shall eat it; with a belt on your waist, your sandals on your feet, and your staff in your hand. So ye shall eat it in haste: it is the LORD's Passover. . . . Now the blood shall be a sign for you on the houses where ye are. And when I see the blood, I will pass over you, and the plague shall not be on you to destroy you, when I strike the land of Egypt" (Exodus 12:3, 5-7, 11, 13).

Leader:

This bone symbolizes the Passover lamb that was killed so the Israelite firstborn might live. The Jewish people no longer eat of the lamb because they have no temple; however, they still celebrate God's grace in providing life for them through the death of another.

People:

We also recognize and celebrate the Lamb of God who was sacrificed once and for all to take away the sin of the world. Praised be his holy name.

Leader (removing the roasted egg from the seder plate and holding it up)*:*

One element that the sages added is the egg, to remind Israel of their responsibility to bring an offering while the temple was standing. Since there is no temple, they can neither offer nor eat this offering. The egg is also said to be a symbol of new life, even of the resurrection.

People (as the leader replaces the egg)*:*

Blessed are you, O Lord our God, King of the universe, who hears the cries of your oppressed people, brings them forth into freedom, and creates a people for yourself.

Leader (holding the remaining half of the middle matzah)*:*

The *matzah* we eat signifies that the bread lacked time to be leavened before the King of kings brought deliverance and redeemed Israel, as it is written:

People:

"And they baked unleavened cakes of the dough which they had brought out of Egypt; for it was not leavened, because they were driven out of Egypt and could not wait, nor had they prepared provisions for themselves" (Exodus 12:39).

Leader (holding the bitter herbs, the maror):

The bitter herbs we eat remind us of the bitterness of slavery in Egypt. As sweet as freedom is now, we must always remember the bitterness of bondage, as it is written:

People:

"[The Egyptians] were in dread of the children of Israel . . . They made their lives bitter with hard labor in brick and mortar and with all kinds of work in the fields" (Exodus 1:12, 14).

Leader (taking up the parsley and the bowl of salt water):

Tonight we dip the *karpas* in salt water, first to remind us of the tears in Egypt, and a second time, to remind us of our sins.

People:

"I am afflicted very much; Revive me, O LORD, according to your word! . . . How sweet are your words to my taste, sweeter than honey to my mouth!" (Psalm 119:107, 103).

THE *HALLEL*

Leader:

Having rehearsed the story of the first Passover, each of us now feels that we have been delivered from Egypt, and we celebrate our freedom. We can join with the thousands of the past and the future in offering praise to God by reading responsively one or more Psalms from Psalm 113-118, the first portion of the *Hallel*.

HAND WASHING

Leader:

Let us all now wash our hands as we set ourselves apart to partake of the Passover meal.

Leader and People:

Blessed are you, O Lord our God, King of the universe, who has set us apart by your word and has made us your people.

BLESSING GOD FOR THE BREAD

Leader:

We are now ready to observe the commandment to eat the *matzah.*

People:

For the sake of the one God, Father of all, and in his presence, may we do it in the name of all of Israel.

Leader (*elevating all three* pieces of matzah *in his hand, with the broken piece remaining in the middle*)*:*

בָּרוּךְ אַתָּה יְיָ אֱלֹהֵינוּ מֶלֶךְ הָעוֹלָם
הַמּוֹצִיא לֶחֶם מִן הָאָרֶץ:

BARUCH ATAH ADONAI, ELOHEYNU, MELECH HA'OLAM, HA MOTZI LECHEM MIN HA'ARETZ.

Blessed are you, O Lord our God, King of the universe, who brings forth bread from the earth.

Leader:

בָּרוּךְ אַתָּה יְיָ אֱלֹהֵינוּ מלֶךְ הָעוֹלָם אֲשֶׁר קִדְשָׁנוּ
בְּמִצְוֹתָיו וְצִוָּנוּ עַל אֲכִילַת מַצָּה:

BARUCH ATAH ADONAI, ELOHEYNU, MELECH HA'OLAM, ASHER KIDSHANU B'MITZVOTAV V'TSIVANU AL ACHILAT MATZAH.

Blessed are you, O Lord our God, King of the universe, who has set us apart us by your commandments and has commanded us concerning the *matzah.*

EATING THE MATZAH

Leader (*holding up only the remaining half of the broken matzah*)*:*

Now we eat the unleavened bread, the bread of haste, so called because our spiritual ancestors left Egypt in haste.

(*Everyone is given a piece of the middle* matzah.)

People:

"You shall eat unleavened bread, the bread of affliction, because you came out of the land of Egypt with great haste, so that all the days of your life you may remember the day of your departure from Egypt" (Deuteronomy 16:3).

(Everyone eats of a portion of the middle matzah.*)*

EATING THE BITTER HERBS

Leader *(holding up the bitter herbs [horseradish] and the top* matzah*):*

Now we eat bitter herbs to remind us of the bitterness of our lives when we were slaves in Egypt.

(Everyone is given a piece of the top matzah.*)*

Leader:

We eat the bitter herbs with the top *matzah* because it was God our Father who commanded, "They are to eat . . . bitter herbs and bread made without yeast" (Exocus 12:8).

People:

"The Egyptians came to dread the Israelites and worked them ruthlessly. They made their lives bitter with hard labor in brick and mortar and with all kinds of work in the fields" (Exodus 1:12, 14).

Leader:

בָּרוּךְ אַתָּה יְיָ, אֱלֹהֵינוּ מֶלֶךְ הָעוֹלָם אֲשֶׁר קִדְּשָׁנוּ בְּמִצְוֹתָיו וְצִוָּנוּ עַל אֲכִילַת מָרוֹר:

BARUKH ATAH ADONAI, ELOHEYNU, MELEKH HA'OLAM, ASHER KIDSHANU B'MITZVOTAV V'TZIVANU AL ACHILAT MAROR.

Blessed are you, O Lord our God, King of the universe, who has set us apart by your commandments and commanded us concerning eating the bitter herbs.

(Everyone dips the matzah *in the bitter herbs and eats it.)*

EATING THE BITTER HERBS
AND CHAROSET TOGETHER

Leader *(taking the third piece of* matzah *and breaking off a large piece for each participant, which in turn is broken in half by the participant):*

We dip in the *maror* for the second time, only now we dip also in the *charoset* to remind us of the sweetness that God always brings to temper the bitterness of life's circumstances. The *charoset*, a mixture of fruit, nuts, and wine, symbolizes the mixture of clay and straw that the Israelites used to make bricks in Egypt. It is red to remind us of the blood of the lamb.

(Everyone dips one olive-sized piece of matzah *in* maror *and another in* charoset, *places them together, and eats them as a sandwich. This is called a Hillel Sandwich after Hillel the Great, who initiated this practice a generation before the time of Jesus.)*

EATING THE MEAL

Leader:

Now let us share in the bounty of God's provision as we eat the Passover meal, rejoicing in our freedom.

(A full meal may be eaten.)

THE DESSERT (*AFIKOMIN*)

Leader:

Before the destruction of the temple, the roasted lamb was the last food that was consumed on Passover; however, since that time, the custom has been to eat the dessert, the *afikomin*, the half of the middle *matzah* that was hidden after the breaking. The *afikomin* substitutes for the Passover lamb.

(The children search for the hidden afikomin, *buried in a linen napkin.)*

Leader:

Now we must redeem the *afikomin*. The gift that we give is a deposit on the full price to be paid in the future. This is a wonderful paradigm for the Holy Spirit that is given to the believer as a deposit on the inheritance of eternal life (2 Corinthians 1:22; 5:5; Ephesians 1:13-14). As we redeem the hidden *afikomin*, we are reminded that our Lord Jesus Christ was resurrected from the dead, just as the ancient blessing declares, "Blessed are you, O Lord our God, King of the universe, who brings forth bread from the earth." Jesus, the bread from heaven, was indeed brought forth from the earth in the resurrection.

(The child who finds the afikomin *receives a reward.)*

Leader:

Called the Promise of the Father, this gift reminds us that God has sent us his Holy Spirit.

People:

"Behold, I send the promise of my Father upon you: but tarry in the city of Jerusalem until you are endued with power from on high" (Luke 24:49).

Leader:

At the time of the exodus, this piece of *matzah*, the *afikomin*, was called the bread of affliction. Indeed, Jesus was afflicted for our sins, but he was raised again the third day according to the Scriptures, ensuring for us eternal life. Just as Israel now eats this bread instead of the paschal lamb, when we eat this bread, we symbolically eat the flesh of the Lamb of God who removes the world's sin.

People:

"Therefore if the Son makes you free, you shall be free indeed" (John 8:36).

(Each participant is given an olive-sized piece of the afikomin.*)*

Leader:

This bread which we now receive, is it not the communion of the body of our Lord Jesus Christ which was broken for us?

People:

"We are all partakers of that one bread." (1 Corinthians 10:17).

Leader:

Take and eat knowing that Christ has died for us, Christ is risen, and Christ is coming again.

(Everyone eats of the afikomin.*)*

GRACE AFTER THE MEAL

Leader:

Blessed are you, O Lord our God, King of the universe, who feeds the whole world with your goodness, with grace, with lovingkindness and tender mercy; you give food to all flesh, for your lovingkindness endures forever. Through your great goodness food has never failed us: O may it not fail us for ever and ever for your great Name's sake, since you nourish and sustain all beings, and do good unto all, and provide food for all your creatures whom you have created. Blessed are you, O Lord, who gives food unto all.

People:

We thank you, O Lord our God, because you gave us an heritage unto our fathers, a desirable, good, and ample land, the covenant and the Torah, and food in plenty. Blessed are you, O Lord, for the land and for the food.

Leader:

Have compassion, O Lord our God, upon Israel thy people, and upon the kingdom of the house of David your anointed: speedily magnify the glory of the Temple, and doubly comfort us. Blessed are you, O Lord, who in your compassion rebuilds Jerusalem. Amen.

People:

Blessed are you, O Lord our God, our Father, our King, who is kind and deals kindly with all; you have dealt kindly, do deal kindly, and will deal kindly with us.

Leader and People:

Let us inherit the day which is altogether good; and make us worthy of the days of the Messiah, and the life of the world to come. He who makes peace in his high places, may he make peace for us and for all Israel, and say ye, Amen.

THE THIRD CUP
THE CUP OF REDEMPTION

Leader:

The third cup of Passover is the Cup of Redemption, so called because God said, "I will redeem you." It celebrated redemption from Egypt. It was this cup that our Lord Jesus shared with his disciples to introduce the New Covenant in his blood by which we celebrate our deliverance from sin.

Leader:

בָּרוּךְ אַתָּה יְיָ אֱלֹהֵינוּ מֶלֶךְ הָעוֹלָם בּוֹרֵא פְּרִי הַגָּפֶן:

BARUKH ATAH, ADONAI, ELOHEYNU, MELEKH HA'OLAM, BOREY PRI HAGAFEN.

Blessed are you, O Lord our God, King of the universe, who creates the fruit of the vine.

Leader:

This cup which we now receive, is it not the blood that our Lord Jesus Christ shed because of our sins?

People:

"This is the cup of the new covenant" (1 Corinthians 11:25).

Leader:

Drink this cup knowing that God was in Christ reconciling the world to himself through the shedding of his blood.

(Everyone drinks of the Cup of Redemption.)

THE GREAT *HALLEL*

(The Great Hallel, Psalm 136, is now read responsively. This was the "hymn"which Jesus and the disciples sang at the end of Passover.)

THE FOURTH CUP
THE CUP OF THANKSGIVING AND CONSUMMATION

Leader:

We now partake of the Cup of Thanksgiving because God said to Israel, "I am the LORD; I will take you as my people, and I will be your God" (Exodus 6:7).

People:

Blessed are you, O Lord our God, King of the universe, who has adopted us as your children and given us the grace through which we call you, *Abba*, Father.

Leader:

This cup is also called the Cup of Consummation, for it is the one to which Jesus referred when he declared, "I will not drink of this fruit of the vine from now on until that day I drink it anew with you in my Father's kingdom" (Matthew 26:29). It speaks to us of the consummation of the relationship to which we have been espoused: "Blessed are those have been called to the marriage supper of the Lamb" (Revelation 19:9).

People:

". . . I have espoused you to one husband, that I may present you as a chaste virgin to Christ" (2 Corinthians 11:2). "The Spirit and the bride say, 'Come.' . . . And whosoever will, let him take of the water of life freely" (Revelation 22:17).

Leader:

This cup is also associated with and is sometimes called the Cup of Elijah, celebrated because of God's promise that he would send the prophet before the coming of the Messiah.We understand from the words of Jesus that John the Baptizer ministered in Elijah's spirit, and we believe that the same spirit is even now bringing restoration in the world, preparing for our Lord's return.

People:

"Even so come, Lord Jesus."

CONCLUSION

Leader:

And now may we join together in praying the prayer our Lord taught his disciples to pray by saying,

Leader and People:

"Our Father in heaven, hallowed be your name. Your kingdom come, your will be done on earth as it is in heaven. Give us today our daily bread, and forgive us our debts, as we also have forgiven our debtors. And lead us not into temptation, but deliver us from the evil one."

Leader:

"The LORD bless you and keep you. The LORD make his face shine upon you and be gracious unto you. The LORD turn his face toward you and give you peace."

"To him who loves us and has freed us from our sins by his blood, and has made us to be a kingdom of priests to serve his God and Father–to him be glory and power for ever and ever! Amen."

As we conclude this Passover, let us shout with all our Jewish brothers around the world:

Leader:

לְשָׁנָה הַבָּאָה בִּירוּשָׁלַיִם:

L'SHANAH HABA'AH B'YERUSHALAYIM.

People:

"Next year in Jerusalem!"

All of the blessings in this ***Christian Passover Haggadah*** are presented in Hebrew and English in ***Passover Blessings and Songs***, an audiocassette produced in Israel by Yuval Shomron (available from Holy Land Gifts–1-800-564-4659).

This cassette also includes songs, in Hebrew and English, such as "We Were Slaves" (*Avadim Hayinu*), "It Is Enough" (*Dayeinu*), "When Israel Went Forth" (*B'tzeit Yisra'el*), "We Were Glad (*Hayeinu Smechim*)," "The Cup of Salvation (*Kos Yeshuot*)," "Hallelujah," "*Adonai Li* (The Lord Is for Me)," and "*Shir Moshe* (Song of Moses)."

Celebrating Passover
with Jesus and the Apostles

Jesus was a fully Torah-observant Jew, the only human being who ever fulfilled all the moral, ethical, and ceremonial requirements of the Law of God. Far from being a radical innovator who started a completely new religion (as much of Christian theology has imagined him to be), Jesus was a faithful and obedient Son who readily affirmed that he had kept all his Father's commandments (John 15:10).

It was only natural, therefore, that one of the last things Jesus did with his disciples here on earth was to celebrate the Passover. "I have eagerly desired to eat this Passover with you before I suffer," he told his followers, "for I tell you, I will not eat it again until it finds fulfillment in the kingdom of God" (Luke 22:15-16, NIV). Jesus was simply doing his duty as a faithful Jew, keeping the explicit commandment his Father had given to his ancestors on the day of the very first Passover: "And this day shall be unto you for a memorial; and ye shall keep it a feast to the Lord throughout your generations; ye shall keep it a feast by an ordinance for ever" (Exodus 12:14, KJV).

When the Passover season approached, Jesus, as a dutiful son of Israel, instructed Peter and John: "Go and make preparations for us to eat the Passover." He even described the advance provision that the Father had made for his final Passover celebration: ". . . a man carrying a jar of water will meet you. Follow him to the house that he enters, and say to the owner of the house, 'The Teacher asks: Where is the guest room, where I may eat the Passover with my disciples?' He will show you a large upper room, all furnished. Make preparations there." (Luke 22:8, 10-12).

PREPARATION FOR PASSOVER

As Jesus had instructed them, "they made ready the Passover." The preparations that had to be made included cleansing the house of leaven, securing the unblemished lamb for the sacrifice, making ready the bitter herbs, baking or acquiring the *matzah* and preparing the wine. We can be certain that the disciples faithfully fulfilled these requirements to ensure that their Lord could rightly celebrate the last of his yearly Passovers.

When Jesus and his apostles assembled in the upper guest room, they did so with all the joy of the Passover season, celebrating the fact that they, like all their other Jewish brothers, had been delivered from Egyptian slavery by God's outstretched arm. Weighing heavily over the assembly, however, was their Master's prediction that he would soon suffer at the hands of the Gentiles (the Romans).

ORDER OF OBSERVANCE

The method of Passover observance had been given in general terms in the Torah itself; however, Israel's sages had expanded upon this outline to establish a *seder* (order) for celebrating the festival. This was a part of the oral tradition that had been passed down from generation to generation. By the time of the Second Temple, virtually all of the celebration that is currently practiced among the Jewish people was already in place in at least a rudimentary form. A generation before the time of Jesus, Hillel, one of Israel's greatest sages, declared that only three things were essential for the proper celebration of Passover: the Passover lamb (*Pesach*), the bitter herbs (*maror*), and the unleavened bread (*matzah*). This teaching was reinforced by Gamliel, a contemporary of Jesus and Paul's teacher. Other elements of celebration had also been added to the traditional order, but these three requirements were the core of the annual remembrance of Passover.

From the evidence present in the Gospel accounts, we can conclude that Jesus and his disciples celebrated the Passover during the final evening of the incarnation by following the order prescribed by the sages that was traditional to their time. Jesus' last Passover supper was not just a casual introduction of the elements of communion. It was a careful exercise in the fulfillment of the divine commandment to remember God's greatest work in Israelite history, a remembrance into which was injected an outline for celebrating God's greatest work in all of human history, the death of the Lamb of God who takes away the sins of the world. It was also done in conformity to the accepted norm for celebration in that day, the sages' *seder*.

Jesus and the disciples likely reclined while eating, probably around a triclinium table (somewhat u-shaped). This was in keeping with the tradition that Passover celebrants were not slaves, who sat or stood while eating, but free men, nobles who reclined while eating.

To begin the Passover, as was the case with all Jewish celebrations, Jesus would have spoken the *Kiddush* blessing, thereby sanctifying the occasion. He would have raised the cup of the fruit of the vine and said, "Blessed are you, O Lord our God, King of the universe, who creates the fruit of the vine."

Jesus also participated in the washing of hands, taking the traditional ceremony for ritual purity to introduce new significance. He washed his disciples feet in the ultimate demonstration of humility and service.

During the course of the meal, Jesus took the unleavened bread (*matzah*) of the Passover meal, the first of three elements essential to Passover observance, and gave it to his disciples to eat, observing that it was his body that was broken for sin. It is significant that Jesus shared the *matzah* with his disciples *during* the meal, since the tradition was that no food was to be eaten after the lamb was consumed.

Jesus also shared the second of the three elements essential to the celebration of Passover: eating bitter herbs. He did this by dipping bread in the bitter herbs in the company of Judas, demonstrating the bitterness of betrayal in the house of his friends.

Jesus and the disciples ate the roasted paschal lamb, the third element essential to the proper celebration of Passover. This was another of the things that his disciples were commissioned to prepare so their Master could eat the Passover that he had so much desired to share with them before his death.

Finally, according to the prescribed order, Jesus took the third cup, the Cup of Redemption (after the meal), blessed God, and enjoined his disciples that as they drank of it, they received the cup of the New Testament in his blood.

Jesus gave no indication that since he was fulfilling the Passover there was no need for its further observance. Indeed, he gave this injunction: ". . . this do in remembrance of me" (Luke 22:19). Paul further encouraged even Gentile believers to observe the festival with the unleavened bread of sincerity and truth because "Christ our Passover is sacrificed for us" (1 Corinthians 5:7). He also observed that when Christians celebrate the Passover, including the remembrance which Jesus commanded, "ye do show forth the Lord's death til he come" (1 Corinthians 11:26).

CELEBRATING TODAY WITH JESUS AND THE APOSTLES

Jesus and the apostles, then, celebrated at least the following elements of the traditional Passover Seder:

The *Kiddush* (Cup of Sanctification)

The Washing of Hands

The Breaking and Eating of Unleavened Bread (when Jesus instituted the bread of communion)

The Washing of the Disciples' Feet

The Dipping and Eating of Bitter Herbs (when Jesus, along with Judas, dipped bread in the bitter herbs)

The Eating of the Passover Lamb (now celebrated by eating the *afikomin*)

The Cup of Redemption (when Jesus instituted the cup of communion)

The Singing of the Hallel (when Jesus and the disciples "sang a hymn)

It is likely, however, that Jesus and the apostles observed not only these but also other portions of the *seder* that certainly predated the Christian era at the very least in embryonic form.

The following ceremony is a Passover Seder that incorporates the elements we know Jesus used when he observed the Passover with his disciples in the Last Supper.

The Last Supper Seder
Featuring
The Order Jesus Observed

Leader:
One of the last things that our Lord Jesus Christ did during his life on earth was to celebrate the Passover. First, he commemorated the Exodus from Egypt in the order (*seder*) that the sages of Israel prescribed. Then, he offered himself as the Paschal Lamb who removes the sin of the world, thereby fulfilling Passover by filling it with new and expanded meaning. In anticipation of this fulfillment, Jesus commanded his disciples to remember his death until he returns by sharing bread and the fruit of the vine in remembrance of his broken body and his shed blood. As we share the Passover in the manner in which Jesus did at the Last Supper, let us rejoice in the eternal life that we have in our Messiah.

THE FIRST CUP: THE CUP OF SANCTIFICATION

Leader:
The Passover story (*Haggadah*) centers on the express fourfold promise of God to Israel. We fill our cups four times to celebrate God's full and free deliverance that brought us out of Egypt. Herein we remember our Father's words:

People:
"I am the Lord; [1] I will bring you out from under the burdens of the Egyptians [*Sanctification*], [2] I will rescue you from their bondage [*Deliverance and Judgment*], and [3] I will redeem you with an outstretched arm and with great judgments [*Redemption*]. [4] I will take you as my people, and I will be your God [*Thanksgiving and Consummation*]" (Exodus 6:6-7).
(Both the leader and the people's cups are partially filled.)

Leader:

בָּרוּךְ אַתָּה יְיָ אֱלֹהֵינוּ מֶלֶךְ הָעוֹלָם בּוֹרֵא פְּרִי הַגָּפֶן:

BARUKH ATAH ADONAI, ELOHEYNU, MELEKH HA'OLAM, BOREY PRI HAGAFEN.

Blessed are you, O Lord our God, King of the universe, who has created the fruit of the vine.

Leader and People:

Blessed are you, O Lord our God, King of the universe, who has chosen us from among all people, and exalted us above all languages and has sanctified us with your commandments, and with love have you given us, O Lord, our God, solemn days for joy, festivals and seasons for gladness: this day of the feast of Unleavened Bread, the season of our freedom: a holy convocation, a memorial of the departure from Egypt: for you have chosen us, and sanctified us above all people: and your holy festivals you have caused us to inherit with joy and gladness. Blessed are you, O Lord, who sanctifies Israel and the seasons.

Blessed are you, O Lord our God, King of the universe, who has preserved us alive, sustained us, and brought us to enjoy this season.

Leader:

We praise you because you fulfill your promises to all your children. Whenever evil ones oppress us, your outstretched hand delivers us and brings us freedom, and we are restored. When the Evil One held us in the clutches of our own sin, you made provision for us through the shedding of the blood of your Son that we could be free, free from sin and inheritors of eternal life.

People:

"I am the LORD: I will bring you out from under the burden of the Egyptians" (Exodus 6:6). "Take this, and divide it among yourselves: for I say unto you, I will not drink of the fruit of the vine, until the kingdom of God shall come" (Luke 22:18); "Therefore if the Son makes you free, you shall be free indeed . . . Sanctify them by your truth, your word is truth . . . and you shall know the truth, and the truth shall make you free" (John 8:36; 17:17; 8:32).

(Everyone drinks of the Cup of Sanctification and Freedom.)

HAND WASHING
Leader:
   The washing of hands is purely ceremonial and not for hygiene. It demonstrates the fact that everyone who comes before God must do so with "clean hands and a pure heart" (Psalm 24:4).
   The lesson in the washing of hands is the fact that we are to be pure before God and submitted one to another in love.
Leader:
   Let us all now wash our hands as we set ourselves apart to partake of the Passover meal.
Leader and People:
   Blessed are you, O Lord our God, King of the universe, who has set us apart by your word and has made us your people.
   (All wash their hands in water.)

BREAKING OF *MATZAH*
Leader:
   In our *seder* we have specially prepared unleavened bread called *matzah*. The Hebrew term for unleavened bread, *matzah*, means "sweet" and is contrasted with the Hebrew word for leavened bread, *chametz*, which means "bitter."
People:
   "O taste and see that the Lord is good" (Psalm 34:8). "How sweet are your words to my taste, sweeter than honey to my mouth!" (Psalm 119:103).
Leader:
   You will notice that in the process of baking this *matzah*, it was pierced in order to ensure that it did not rise from incipient yeast. In the baking process brown stripes are created along these pierced rows. This brings vividly to our minds the suffering of our Messiah.
People:
   "He was wounded for our transgressions, he was bruised for our iniquities . . . and by his stripes we are healed" (Isaiah 53:5); ". . . they pierced my hands and my feet" (Psalm 22:16); ". . . they shall look on me whom they have pierced . . ." (Zechariah 12:10).
Leader:
   The sages have prescribed that in partaking of the unleavened

bread, one of the three essential elements of the Passover *seder*, be received from three pieces of *matzah* separated in the folds of a napkin or in the three compartments of a specially designed bag. The three pieces of *matzah*, called by the sages "Unity," represent Abraham, Isaac, and Jacob as well as the three divisions of the Hebrew Scriptures: *Torah* (Law), *Nevi'im* (Prophets), and *Ketuvim* (Writings). They also represent the three levels of divine service in Israel: the Priests, the Levites, and the people of Israel.

It is also said that the three pieces of *matzah* can be traced to the three measures of flour which Abraham asked Sarah to bake when the angels visited him, according to tradition, on the eve of Passover. Abraham's instruction to Sarah to "be quick" in taking three measures of flour and making cakes parallels God's instruction on Passover that the Israelites eat the *matzah* in haste.

Many early Jewish Christians celebrated the Passover with three pieces of *matzah* to represent the three elements of the one God: Father, Son, and Holy Spirit. Furthermore, it is the middle of the three pieces of *matzah* that is broken into two pieces, symbolizing the human body of Jesus that was broken for sin.

All *matzah* on Passover is called the Bread of Affliction. It was the bread that we ate at the time of our greatest suffering in Egypt. It also symbolizes the broken body of Jesus who was afflicted when the Father placed upon him the sins of us all.

People:

"I am the living bread which came down from heaven. If anyone eats of this bread, he will live for ever" (John 6:51). "For indeed Christ our Passover was sacrificed for us" (1 Corinthians 5:7). "For he was cut off from the land of the living; for the transgressions of my people he was stricken" (Isaiah 53:8); however, he was discovered to be alive, resurrected in a glorious body (Philippians 3:21).

BLESSING GOD FOR THE BREAD

Leader:

We are now ready to observe the commandment to eat the *matzah*.

People:

For the sake of the one God, Father of all, and in his presence, may we do it in the name of all of Israel.

Leader (*taking all three* matzot *in his hand*):

בָּרוּךְ אַתָּה יְיָ אֱלֹהֵינוּ מֶלֶךְ הָעוֹלָם
הַמּוֹצִיא לֶחֶם מִן הָאָרֶץ:

BARUCH ATAH ADONAI, ELOHEYNU, MELECH HA'OLAM, HA MOTZI LECHEM MIN HA'ARETZ.

Blessed are you, O Lord our God, King of the universe, who brings forth bread from the earth.

בָּרוּךְ אַתָּה יְיָ אֱלֹהֵינוּ מֶלֶךְ הָעוֹלָם אֲשֶׁר קִדְּשָׁנוּ
בְּמִצְוֹתָיו וְצִוָּנוּ עַל אֲכִילַת מַצָּה:

BARUCH ATAH ADONAI, ELOHEYNU, MELECH HA'OLAM, ASHER KIDSHANU B'MITZVOTAV V'TSIVANU AL ACHILAT MATZAH.

Blessed are you, O Lord our God, King of the universe, who has set us apart us by your commandments and has commanded us concerning the *matzah.*

EATING THE *MATZAH*

(This is the Bread of Communion.)

Leader (*holding up the middle* matzah *and breaking it*):

Now we eat the unleavened bread, the bread of haste, so called because our ancestors left Egypt in such haste that they had no time for their bread to rise.

People:

"You shall eat unleavened bread, the bread of affliction, because you came out of the land of Egypt with great haste, so that all the days of your life you may remember the day of your departure from Egypt" (Deuteronomy 16:3).

(All are given olive-sized pieces of the middle matzah.*)*

Leader:

At the time of the exodus *matzah* was called the bread of affliction. Indeed, Jesus was afflicted for our sins, but he was raised again the third day according to the Scriptures, ensuring for us eternal life. Just as Israel now eats this bread instead of the paschal lamb, when we eat this bread, we symbolically eat the flesh of the Lamb of God who takes away the sin of the world.

People:

"Therefore if the Son makes you free, you shall be free indeed" (John 8:36).

(All eat of the matzah.*)*

WASHING THE DISCIPLES' FEET

Our Lord Jesus not only washed his own hands during the Passover celebration, but at the end of the supper, he demonstrated the ultimate act of humility in washing the feet of the twelve disciples who shared that Last Passover with him. "After that he poured water into a basin, and began to wash the disciples' feet" (John 13:5). As we remember this demonstration of servanthood that our Lord gave on the night of his last Passover, we affirm our commitment to serve one another in love.

EATING THE BITTER HERBS

Leader *(holding up the bitter herbs, usually horseradish and the top* matzah*):*

Now we eat bitter herbs to remind us of the bitterness of our lives when we were slaves in Egypt and of the bitterness that our Lord experienced when he was betrayed by one of his disciples.

People:

"The Egyptians came to dread the Israelites and worked them ruthlessly. They made their lives bitter with hard labor in brick and mortar and with all kinds of work in the fields" (Exodus 1:12-14).

"After he had said this, Jesus was troubled in spirit and testified, 'I tell you the truth, one of you is going to betray me. . . . It is the one to whom I will give this piece of bread when I have dipped it in the dish.' Then, dipping the piece of bread, he gave it to Judas Iscariot, son of Simon" (John 13:21, 26).

Leader:

בָּרוּךְ אַתָּה יְיָ אֱלֹהֵינוּ מֶלֶךְ הָעוֹלָם אֲשֶׁר קִדְּשָׁנוּ
בְּמִצְוֹתָיו וְצִוָּנוּ עַל אֲכִילַת מָרוֹר:

Barukh atah Adonai, Eloheynu, Melekh ha'olam, asher kidshanu b'mitzvotav v'tzivanu al achilat maror.

Blessed are you, O Lord our God, King of the universe, who has set us apart by your word and commanded us concerning eating the bitter herbs.

(Everyone dips a piece of matzah *in the bitter herbs and eats it.)*

EATING THE PASSOVER MEAL
(Jesus and the apostles at the Passover meal, including the lamb. A meal may be eaten, or the afikomin *may be substituted.)*

THE THIRD CUP: THE CUP OF REDEMPTION
(Every fills the cup. This is the Cup of Communion.)

Leader:

The third cup of Passover is the Cup of Redemption, so called because God said, "I will redeem you." It celebrated redemption from Egypt. It was this cup that our Lord Jesus shared with his disciples to introduce the New Covenant in his blood by which we celebrate our deliverance from sin.

Leader:

בָּרוּךְ אַתָּה יְיָ אֱלֹהֵינוּ מֶלֶךְ הָעוֹלָם בּוֹרֵא פְּרִי הַגָּפֶן:

Barukh atah, Adonai, Eloheynu, Melekh ha'olam, borey pri hagafen.

Blessed are you, O Lord our God, King of the universe, who creates the fruit of the vine.

Leader:

This cup which we now receive, is it not the blood that our Lord Jesus Christ shed because of our sins?

People:

"This is the cup of the new covenant" (1 Corinthians 11:25).

Leader:

Drink this cup knowing that God was in Christ reconciling the world to himself through the shedding of his blood.

(All drink of the Cup of Redemption.)

THE FOURTH CUP: THE CUP OF THANKSGIVING AND CONSUMMATION

(Jesus declared that he would not drink of this cup until the kingdom. We recognize it as the promise of his second coming.)

Leader:

This cup is called the Cup of Consummation, for it is the one to which Jesus referred when he declared, "I will not drink of this fruit of the vine from now on until that day I drink it anew with you in my Father's kingdom" (Matthew 26:29). It speaks to us of the consummation of the relationship to which we have been espoused, the marriage supper of the Lamb: "Blessed are those have been called to the marriage supper of the Lamb" (Revelation 19:9).

People:

". . . I have espoused you to one husband, that I may present you as a chaste virgin to Christ" (2 Corinthians 11:2). "The Spirit and the bride say, 'Come.' . . . And whosoever will, let him take of the water of life freely" (Revelation 22:17).

Leader:

This cup is also associated with and is sometimes called the Cup of Elijah, celebrated because of God's promise that he would send the prophet before the coming of the Messiah. We understand from the words of Jesus that John the Baptizer ministered in Elijah's spirit, and we believe that the same spirit is even now bringing restoration in the world, preparing for our Lord's return.

People:

"Even so come, Lord Jesus."

(Since Jesus said he would not drink of this cup until the kingdom, we reserve this cup to be drunk with him at that day.)

THE *HALLEL*

The Hallel Psalms (113-118) may be read responsively. From this collection of Psalms was selected the "hymn" which Jesus and the disciples sang as they concluded the Passover and left the Upper

Room for the Garden of Gethsemane. (The Great Hallel, Psalm 136 is given here.)

Leader:

Oh, give thanks to the LORD, for *He is* good! For His mercy *endures* forever.

People:

Oh, give thanks to the God of gods! For His mercy *endures* forever.

Leader:

Oh, give thanks to the Lord of lords! For His mercy *endures* forever:

People:

To Him who alone does great wonders, For His mercy *endures* forever;

Leader:

To Him who by wisdom made the heavens, For His mercy *endures* forever;

People:

To Him who laid out the earth above the waters, For His mercy *endures* forever;

Leader:

To Him who made great lights, For His mercy *endures* forever —

People:

The sun to rule by day, For His mercy *endures* forever;

Leader:

The moon and stars to rule by night, For His mercy *endures* forever.

People:

To Him who struck Egypt in their firstborn, For His mercy *endures* forever;

Leader:

And brought out Israel from among them, For His mercy *endures* forever;

People:

With a strong hand, and with an outstretched arm, For His mercy *endures* forever;

Leader:
To Him who divided the Red Sea in two, For His mercy *endures* forever;
People:
And made Israel pass through the midst of it, For His mercy *endures* forever;
Leader:
But overthrew Pharaoh and his army in the Red Sea, For His mercy *endures* forever;
People:
To Him who led His people through the wilderness, For His mercy *endures* forever;
Leader:
To Him who struck down great kings, For His mercy *endures* forever;
People:
And slew famous kings, For His mercy *endures* forever —

"GOING OUT"
Leader:
After Jesus and the disciples concluded their singing of the Hallel Psalms, they "went out."

Now, beloved, go out into the world in peace, knowing that he who has purchased your redemption will present you unto himself in glory at his coming.

The Lord bless you and keep you. The Lord cause his face to shine upon you and be gracious unto you. The Lord turn his face toward you and give you peace, in the name of the Prince of Peace, the Lord Jesus Christ, to whom be glory and praise forever and ever. Amen.

Passover and Holy Communion

Holy Communion has long been one of the most sacred of celebrations in the Christian church. Though it has taken many forms and has been celebrated in various manners, the core of this ceremony is derived from the Passover observance of ancient Israel. Virtually every Christian congregation or community, therefore, shares in a rich legacy from biblical and Second Temple Judaism.

The one ceremony that Jesus instructed his disciples to observe was that of partaking of bread and the fruit of the vine as a means of remembering his death until his second coming. From the very earliest of church history, Christians were found faithfully fulfilling this imperative.

Following the order which Jesus established on the night of the Last Supper, Paul gave specific instructions to the church: "For I received from the Lord that which I also delivered to you: that the Lord Jesus on the *same* night in which He was betrayed took bread; and when He had given thanks, He broke *it* and said, 'Take, eat; this is My body which is broken for you; do this in remembrance of Me.' In the same manner *He* also *took* the cup after supper, saying, 'This cup is the new covenant in My blood. This do, as often as you drink *it,* in remembrance of Me' " (1 Corinthians 11:23-26).

The immediate antecedent for communion in the earliest church was clearly the Passover Seder. The earliest Christians recognized profound spiritual significance in the death, burial, and resurrection of Jesus around the time of Passover, and they translated that meaning into their ongoing celebration of the biblical festival that was so much a part of their lives and tradition.

The practice of sharing bread and wine in acts of worship

was a long-standing tradition among the Hebrew peoples, dating at least to the time of Melchizedek, the king-priest of Salem, who brought forth bread and wine to celebrate with Abraham. It continued throughout antiquity, practiced by prophets and kings, by peasants and wise men.

Sharing bread and wine was also manifest in the weekly celebration of the *Shabbat* (Sabbath) in the context of the Jewish home. Just as the annual Passover was primarily a family celebration, so the weekly *Shabbat* was focused in the family.

Great flexibility is a feature of the Hebraic practice of worship. It is for this reason that various forms may be adopted for celebration of Passover and communion. Both may be combined into one as in the earliest church. What is important is not punctilious, legalistic observance, but remembrance of the pivotal events of biblical history, the Exodus and the death, burial, resurrection, and ascension of Jesus Christ, *Yeshua HaMashiach*.

The following is a liturgy for Holy Communion that incorporates elements of the synagogal liturgy in which Jesus and the apostles participated throughout their lifetimes. It includes parts of what was called "The Prayer" in the synagogue worship experience, and it uses ancient language patterns for other parts of the ceremony, including the blessings for the bread and the fruit of the vine.

This ceremony is designed to be an introduction to liturgical or sacramental congregations into the richness of the Hebraic heritage that the church has lost for some seventeen centuries. It represents an enriching of traditional Christian ceremony with language and forms in which Jesus and his Jewish family and community worshipped in home, synagogue, and temple.

New Covenant Passover

A Liturgy for Holy Communion

PRELUDE

PROCESSIONAL

GREETING:

Leader:
Peace be unto you. The Lord be with you.

People:
And also with you.

CALL TO WORSHIP:

Leader:
Christ our Passover has been sacrificed for us: Christ has died; Christ is risen; Christ is coming again.

People:
Therefore, let us observe the Festival of Passover.

COLLECT:

Leader:
Almighty God, unto whom all hearts are open, all desires known, and from whom no secrets are hidden, cleanse the thoughts of our hearts by the inspiration of your Holy Spirit, that we may perfectly love you and worthily magnify your holy Name, through Jesus Christ our Lord. Amen.

ACT OF PRAISE: *(Congregation standing)*

(The Act of Praise is modified from the ancient Jewish Amidah *prayer for festivals, a form of which Jesus and the apostles prayed during corporate worship in their synagogues.)*

Leader:
O Lord, open our lips, and our mouths shall declare your praise.

Leader and People:

Blessed are you, O Lord our God and God of our fathers, Abraham, Isaac, and Jacob; the great, mighty and revered God, the Most High God, who bestows loving kindnesses, and is Master of all things; who remembers the pious deeds of the patriarchs, and in love will bring redemption to their children's children for your Name's sake.

Leader:

O King, Helper, Savior, and Shield. Blessed are you, O Lord, the Shield of Abraham.

Leader and People:

You, O Lord, are mighty forever, you revive the dead, you are mighty to save. You sustain the living with loving kindness, revive the dead with great mercy, support the falling, heal the sick, free the bound, and keep your faith to them that sleep in the dust. Who is like unto you, Lord of mighty acts, and who resembles you, O King, who orders death and restores life, and causes salvation to spring forth? Yes, faithful are you to revive the dead. Blessed are you, O Lord, who resurrects the dead.

Leader:

We will sanctify your Name in the world even as they sanctify it in the highest heavens, as it is written by the hand of thy prophet: And they called one unto another and said,

People:

Holy, holy, holy is the Lord of hosts: the whole earth is full of his glory.

Leader:

Those over against them say,

People:

Blessed be the glory of the Lord from his place.

Leader:

And in thy Holy Word it is written, saying

People:

The Lord shall reign forever; your God, O Zion, unto all generations. Praise ye the Lord.

Leader:

Unto all generations we will declare your greatness, and to all eternity we will proclaim your holiness. Your praise, O Lord our God, shall not depart from our mouth forever, for you are a great and holy God and King. Blessed are you, O Lord, the holy God.

Leader:

You favor man with knowledge and teach mortals understanding.

People:

You have favored us with a knowledge of your Word and have taught us to perform your will. You have made a distinction, O Lord our God, between holy and profane, between light and darkness, between Israel and the nations, between the Sabbath and the six working days. O our Father, our King, grant that the days which are approaching us may begin for us in peace and that we may be withheld from all sin and cleansed from all iniquity and cleave to the reverence of your name.

Leader and People:

Blessed are you, O Lord our God, who sanctifies Israel and the festive seasons.

Leader:

Accept, O Lord our God, your people Israel and their prayer; restore the service to the inner sanctuary of your house; receive in love and favor both the offerings of Israel and their prayer; and may the worship of your people Israel be ever acceptable unto you.

People:

Our God and God of our fathers! May our remembrance ascend, come, and be accepted before you, with the remembrance of our fathers, of Messiah the Son of David your servant, of Jerusalem your holy city, and of all your people, the house of Israel, bringing deliverance and well-being, grace, loving kindness and mercy, life and peace on this day of the Feast of Unleavened Bread.

Leader and People:

Remember us, O Lord our God, thereon for our well-being; be mindful of us for blessing, and save us unto life: by your promise of salvation and mercy, spare us, and be gracious unto us;

have mercy upon us, and save us; for our eyes are bent upon you, because you are a gracious and merciful God and King. Let our eyes behold your return in mercy to Zion. Blessed are you, O Lord, who restores your divine presence unto Zion.

Leader:

We give thanks unto you, for you are the Lord our God and the God of our fathers for ever and ever; you are the Rock of our lives, the Shield of our salvation through every generation.

People:

We will give thanks unto you and declare your praise for our lives which are committed unto your hand, and for our souls which are in your charge, and for your miracles, which are daily with us, and for your wonders and your benefits, which are wrought at all times, evening, morn, and noon. You who are all good, whose mercies fail not, you, merciful God, whose loving kindnesses never cease, we have ever hoped in you.

Leader:

Grant peace, welfare, blessing, grace, loving kindness, and mercy unto us and unto all Israel, your people. Bless us, O our Father, even all of us together, with the light of your countenance; for by the light of your countenance you have given us, O Lord our God, the Word of life, loving kindness and righteousness, blessing, mercy, life, and peace; and may it be good in your sight to bless your people Israel at all times and in every hour with your peace.

Blessed are you, O Lord, who blesses your people Israel with peace.

Leader and People:

O my God! guard my tongue from evil and my lips from speaking guile. Let the words of my mouth and the meditation of my heart be acceptable before you, O Lord, my Rock and my Redeemer. He who makes peace in his high places, may he make peace for us and for all Israel. Amen.

(Songs of praise may also be used to conclude the Act of Praise.)

EXAMINATION:

Leader:

As we prepare to partake of this Feast of the Lord, we are admonished in the Holy Scriptures, "Let a man examine himself, for if we judge ourselves, we should not be judged."
(Silence)

CONFESSION:

Leader:

Most holy and merciful Father, we confess to you and to one another that we have sinned against you by what we have done and by what we have left undone. We have not loved you with our whole heart and mind and strength, and we have not loved our neighbors as ourselves; therefore, we have not had the mind of Christ, and we have grieved you by not using your gifts, by wandering from your ways, and by forgetting your love. Forgive us, we pray you, most merciful Father, as we tarry before you and one another. Renew in us the grace and strength of your Holy Spirit and help us to be perfect in your sight, for the sake of Jesus Christ our Lord and Savior. Amen.

Leader:

My little children, if any man sin, we have an advocate with the Father, Jesus Christ the righteous. Let us, therefore, pray:

Leader and People:

Our Father which art in heaven, hallowed be thy name. Thy kingdom come. Thy will be done in earth as it is in heaven. Give us this day our daily bread, and forgive us our debts as we forgive our debtors. And lead us not into temptation, but deliver us from evil. Amen.

DECLARATION OF PARDON:

Leader:

Blessed are they whose iniquities are forgiven, and whose sins are covered.

DOXOLOGY: *(Congregation standing)*

SERMON: *(Appropriate sermon)*

AFFIRMATION OF FAITH: *(Congregation standing)*

Leader:

Hear, O Israel, the Lord our God, the Lord is one.

People:

And you shall love the Lord your God with all your heart, and with all your soul, and with all your might. And these words, which I command you this day, shall be upon your heart: and you shall teach them diligently unto your children, and shall talk of them when you sit in your house, and when you walk by the way, and when you lie down, and when you rise up.

Leader and People:

I believe with perfect faith in one God, the Father Almighty, maker of heaven and earth and of all things visible and invisible.

I believe with perfect faith in the Lord Jesus Christ, *Yeshua HaMashiach*, the only begotten Son of God, begotten of his Father before all worlds, God of God, begotten of one substance with the Father; by whom all things were made; who for us men and for our salvation came down from heaven and became incarnate by the Holy Spirit of the virgin Mary and was made man; who was crucified also for us under Pontius Pilate; who suffered and was buried and the third day rose again according to the Scriptures; who ascended into heaven and now sits on the right hand of the Father; and who will come again in power and great glory to judge both the living and the dead in His everlasting kingdom.

I believe with perfect faith in the Holy Spirit, the Lord and giver of life who proceeds from the Father and the Son, who with the Father and the Son together is worshipped and glorified; who spoke by the prophets; and who indwells the hearts of the believers, imparting His gifts and graces.

I believe with perfect faith in the forgiveness of sins, in the one universal and apostolic congregation of believers, in the resurrection of the body, and in eternal life in the world to come.

HYMN OF WORSHIP: *(An appropriate hymn may be used.)*

OFFERTORY: *(Congregation seated)*

Leader:

Beloved in the Messiah, the Holy Scriptures tell us that after Jesus arose from the dead, he appeared to his disciples and was known to them in the breaking of the bread. Come then to the joyful feast of the Lord. Let us prepare his table with the offerings of our life and labor.

ANTHEM:

(As the offering is received from the congregation, the leaders of the congregation may bring to the the altar the gifts of bread and wine, followed by the offerings that are received from the people.)

OFFERTORY PRAYER:

Leader:

Heavenly Father, receive, we pray you, these offerings of our labor. May Yeshua, our great High Priest, be present with us as he was among his disciples, and may we discern his body in the breaking of the bread and his blood in the sharing of the cup. To you be praise and glory with your Son, our Savior, and the Holy Spirit, now and forever. Amen.

DANCE: *(An appropriate interpretive dance may be performed.)*

SACRIFICE OF PRAISE AND THANKSGIVING:

Leader:

We are told in the Holy Scriptures that we are built up a spiritual house, a holy priesthood to offer up spiritual sacrifices, acceptable to God by Jesus Christ. Let us, therefore, offer a sacrifice of praise unto God:

Leader:

Our holy Father, almighty and eternal God, we give you thanks always and everywhere, through Jesus Christ your Son our Lord. We bless you for your continual love and care for every creature. We praise you for forming us in your image, and calling us to be your people. Though we rebelled against your love, you did not abandon us in our sin, but sent to us prophets and teachers to lead us into the way of salvation and to teach us to remember your wondrous works through days and feasts of memorial.

Above all, we thank you that in the fullness of time, you gave us the gift of your only begotten Son, who is the way, the truth, and the life. We thank you that He took upon Himself our nature, and by His miraculous birth, His sinless life, His atoning death, and His glorious resurrection, He became our Passover to deliver us from the bondage of sin and death into the hope of everlasting life. We praise you that He now reigns with you in glory and ever lives to intercede for us.

We thank you for the Holy Spirit who leads us into truth, defends us in adversity, and unites us out of every people into one holy and universal church. Therefore, with the whole company of saints here assembled we worship and glorify you, Eternal God, most holy, and we say with joy:

Leader and People:

Christ our Passover is sacrificed for us. His death we proclaim. His resurrection we declare. His coming we await.

BLESSING GOD FOR THE BREAD:

Leader:

Blessed are you, O Lord our God, King of the universe, who brings forth bread from the earth to nourish our bodies, and who brought forth the true bread from heaven to strengthen and establish our souls. We thank you that in the hour when you had no pleasure in sacrifices and offerings, you did prepared a body of flesh for your only begotten Son and made him a little lower than the angels that he might taste death for all men. We thank you that he was tempted in all things like as we, yet without sin, that the captain of our salvation was made perfect through suffering, and that he put away sin by the sacrifice of himself. Now, we remember the New Covenant Passover as we break this bread in which, by the authority of your holy Word, we discern the body of Yeshua the Messiah which was broken for us. May they who receive this bread be strengthened in their communion with one another and with our Lord Jesus Christ. Amen.

BREAKING OF THE BREAD:

Leader:

The bread which we break, is it not the communion of the body of Christ?

People:

Because there is one bread, we who are many are one body in the Messiah, for we all partake of that one spiritual bread.

BLESSING GOD FOR THE CUP:

Leader:

Blessed are you, O Lord our God, King of the universe, who creates the fruit of the vine to confirm and make glad our bodies, and who brought forth the true wine from heaven to indwell our hearts and comfort our spirits. We thank you that when the blood of bulls and of goats could not make the worshippers perfect, our Savior entered in once into the holy place by his own blood and obtained eternal redemption for us. Now according to his commandment, we remember the New Covenant Passover as we share this cup in which, by the authority of your holy Word, we discern the blood of Yeshua the Messiah which was shed for the remission of our sins. May they who receive this cup be strengthened through the fellowship of the Spirit in the union of the body of Christ and the risen Lord. Amen.

RECOGNITION OF THE CUP:

Leader:
The cup which we bless, is it not the communion of the blood of Christ?

People:
The cup which we drink is the New Covenant in the blood of the Messiah.

PRAYER FOR COMMUNICANTS:

Leader:
Heavenly Father, we pray now that all those who receive of this Passover may be one in communion with the Messiah and one in communion with each other. Grant that they remain faithful in love and hope until that perfect feast with our Lord in the joy of His eternal kingdom. Amen.

COMMUNION:
(The communicants may receive the elements of communion in a variety of ways according to the tradition of the congregation.)

HYMN OF CONFIRMATION:
(An appropriate hymn confirming the efficacy of the blood of Christ to atone for sin may be sung.)

PRAYER OF THANKSGIVING: *(Congregation Standing)*

Leader and People:
Almighty and everlasting God, we give you thanks for receiving our sacrifice of praise and thanksgiving, and for feeding us

with the spiritual food of the body and blood of our Savior Jesus Christ. Strengthen us ever with your Holy Spirit that we may serve you in faith and love, by word and deed, until we come to the joy of your eternal kingdom; through Yeshua HaMashiach, our Lord, who lives and reigns with you and the same Holy Spirit, now and forever. Amen.

HYMNS OF FELLOWSHIP:

(Songs stressing the unity of the body of Christ may be sung, and appropriate gestures of fellowship may be exchanged among the communicants.)

HYMN OF EXPECTATION:

(A hymn emphasizing the coming of the Messiah may be sung.)

BENEDICTION:
Leader:

Now the God of peace, that brought again from the dead our Lord Jesus, that great shepherd of the sheep, through the blood of the everlasting covenant, make you perfect in every good work to do His will, working in you that which is well pleasing in His sight. The Lord bless you and keep you. The Lord make his face to shine upon you and be gracious unto you. The Lord lift up his countenance upon you and give you peace, through Yeshua HaMashiach, our Lord; to whom be glory for ever and ever, world without end. Amen.

THE DISMISSAL:

Leader:

Go out into the world in peace. Be strong and of good courage. Hold fast what is good. Love and serve the Lord, rejoicing in the power of the Holy Spirit.

RECESSIONAL

POSTLUDE

Shall We Now Observe the Festival?

Jewish and Christian leaders, both in history and in the present day, offer considerable objection to Christian observance of the Passover. It seems that neither official Judaism nor official Christianity is very tolerant of Christians who confuse and confound the clear delineation between these two faiths by attempting to observe the traditional Passover, with or without including the Calvary experience.

CHRISTIAN CONCERNS

Most Christian objection to Passover observance is based on ecclesiastical anti-Judaism that developed after the church's first century. Before the church fully opened the door to the Gentiles at the Jerusalem Council, the vast majority of its communicants were Jews; therefore, there was no question as to whether or not Christians should observe Passover. Its celebration was a significant part of the Jewish heritage upon which the early Jewish leaders of the church had founded a faith and polity that recognized Jesus as the fulfillment of the messianic expectation of his people and as the Savior of the world.

As Gentiles came to prominence in the church, they were influenced by traditions which they had brought with them and by pressures from the political powers of the day to disassociate themselves from the Jews and things Jewish. At the same time a controversy raged in the church over whether or not complete obedience to the law of Moses was essential to salvation in addition to faith in Jesus. Of particular concern was the practice of circumcision, whether it should be physically enforced on new converts to this Judeo-Christianity or whether the circumcision of the heart that God had described to Moses, Jeremiah, and Paul was sufficient without the physical procedure.

In some of Paul's writings, he openly attacked that part of the Jewish community (both in traditional Judaism and in the church) that believed that salvation resulted from submission to and ritual observance of God's law. This social criticism, an intramural exercise among fellow Jews, was misunderstood and generalized by later Gentile church leaders.

Rather than maintain Paul's balanced position on the interrelationship of Christian faith and the law, subsequent church leaders adopted an increasingly antinomian posture, ultimately insisting that Christians have nothing in common with Jews and Judaism. This was particularly true in relationship to ecclesiastical holy days which had been changed from their original first-century construct to accommodate the various societies into which the Christian faith had expanded. Passages such as Colossians 2:16-17 were enlisted to assure Christians that all "Jewish" holy days and sabbaths had been abandoned by the church.

Additionally, virtually all of the Christian church, including the reform movements that began in the sixteenth century and afterward, maintained a supersessionist view toward Jews and Judaism which asserted that Christianity had forever replaced Judaism in God's economy of salvation and that Christians had forever replaced the Jewish people who had been cursed because of their rejection of Jesus.

Having been ripped from its moorings, Christianity drifted on the tide of human tradition, often swirling in the maelstrom of a pagan-based world view that allowed such violent conduct toward the Jewish people. In this kind of environment, it was unthinkable that a Christian would celebrate a "Jewish" festival, including the Passover. Even today, in an age of enlightenment, much of the church is wary of any involvement in "Jewish" practices.

Growing numbers of Christians, however, are rejecting these historical arguments and are rediscovering Christianity's Jewish connection. They are saying to themselves, "If it was right for Jesus and the apostles, it must be right for me." They are embracing teachings and practices that were clearly a part of the first century church's system of praise, worship, and service. And, they are discovering rewarding and fulfilling experiences as they immerse themselves in this clearly biblical and "New Testament" heritage.

CHRISTIAN PASSOVER—A JEWISH INTERPRETATION

Both Jews and Christians need to recognize the fact that Christian understanding of prophecies and practices in the Hebrew Scriptures rests on interpretations of those Scriptures by Jews of the first century who came to see in Jesus of Nazareth the Messiah of Israel. Jesus himself was a Torah-observant Jew. All of the apostles on whom the church was built were Torah-observant Jews. Virtually the entire constituency of the church's first decade were Jews who were faithful to the law. Indeed, many of their number were and continued to be Pharisees (Acts 15:5) and temple priests (Acts 6:7). As Jews, they had a clear and distinct right to interpret their Scriptures apart from any overarching dogma or systematic theology imposed upon them by another part of the traditional Jewish community, for no one branch of Judaism was dominant at that time.

Christian interpretations of the Passover and its manifestation in the death and resurrection of Jesus are established on the solid rock of *Jewish* interpretation. These Jewish followers of Jesus celebrated the Passover *seder* traditions of their day, imbuing each part with additional meaning from the life, death, resurrection, and ascension of Jesus. When the early Jewish leaders of the Christian church interpreted the Passover events allegorically as pointing to Jesus, they did so on the basis of Jewish hermeneutics.Later Gentile Christians' allegorical interpretations of the Exodus Passover events merely expanded upon the foundation that their Jewish predecessors had laid. These ideas, then, were birthed in the fertile hearts of observant Jews: Jesus and his apostles. They are, therefore, Jewish interpretations, not Gentile interpolations that can be casually dismissed as lacking authenticity.

NATURALIZED CITIZENS

One of the key concepts that was advanced when the Jewish founders of the Christian church purposed to open the door of faith to the Gentiles was that this action was also a fulfillment of the Hebrew Scriptures, which had predicted that Israel's light would be carried to the nations of the world (Isaiah 42:6; 49:6; cf. Luke 2:32; Acts 13:47). It was also a cardinal principle that all those Gentiles who were added to the church were, in effect, added to the commonwealth of Israel (Ephesians 2:12-16) or the tabernacle of David (Acts 15:15-18), albeit on the basis of less restrictive initiation requirements.

The bottom line is that all the Gentiles who came to faith in Jesus were considered by their Jewish brethren to have been grafted into God's family tree of salvation and covenant relationship (the theme of Romans 11). They were also considered to have become naturalized citizens in the commonwealth or nation of Israel, a teaching clearly set forth in Ephesians 2. They were "no more strangers and foreigners" but "fellow citizens with the saints and of the same body." Even in ancient Israel, a proselyte was to be considered as though he had been born to Jewish parents.

Paul made this clear in 1 Corinthians 10:1 when, writing specifically to Gentile Christians, he declared: "For I do not want you to be ignorant of the fact, brothers, that *our* forefathers were all under the cloud and that they all passed through the sea" (emphasis supplied). Coupled with his declaration to Gentile believers in Romans 4:12, 16 that Abraham is "the father of us all [Jew and Gentile]," it is clear that the apostle considered the Gentiles who had come to faith in the Messiah to be children of the patriarch, Abraham.

With this in mind, it is only natural that there is a longing in the heart of Christians to rediscover the roots of their faith, to find their way back home. Clearly Gentiles by birth, they have been added to the nation of Israel by faith in Jesus. As fellow citizens with the saints of Israel, they are entitled to the entire heritage of God's chosen people. If one immigrates into a nation of the modern world, he can either remain a foreigner or he can go through the process of naturalization. In the United States when one takes the oath of allegiance, he is as much a citizen as the person whose ancestors signed the Declaration of Independence, and he has virtually the same rights. Virtually every other nation has just such a memorial day for its statehood in which naturalized citizens share equally with the native born.

Passover is the yearly memorial of the liberation of Israel, the event that set them on the path toward Sinai and their incorporation as God's chosen nation of priests. It is foundational to Judaism, but it is also foundational to Christianity, for if there had been no Passover, there would have been no nation of Israel to have produced Jesus, nor would there have been a nation of Israel into whom Gentile believers could be added as naturalized citizens.

To Celebrate or Not to Celebrate

Should Christians celebrate Passover? This is a legitimate question to which much of the church and most of Judaism have said no. But, the answer for believers must be what is given in Holy Scripture.

Should Christians celebrate Passover? When we remain faithful to the Bible, the answer is clear and unequivocal: "Because Christ our Passover has been sacrificed for us; therefore, let us observe the festival [Passover and Unleavened Bread] . . . with the unleavened bread of sincerity and truth." This directive is from a Christian apostle who even then was still a Jewish rabbi, and it was given to Gentiles. What could possibly be more apparent?

The next question is, How should Christians observe the Passover? Again, the Bible gives a clear answer. What better example could we have than that of our Lord Jesus himself? According to the Gospels, he celebrated the Passover with his disciples in the traditional *seder* that the sages had prescribed for his time. The core of the modern *seder* predates the time of Christ and was the order which Jesus employed in the Last Supper. Christians are free to imitate Jesus' way of life at any time; however, they are bound to no specific ritual for their salvation. Freedom in the Messiah permits great flexibility of practice.

Should any remain confused, Paul gives the liturgical order for recognizing Calvary in the Passover celebration: "For I received from the Lord that which I also delivered to you: that the Lord Jesus on the same night in which He was betrayed took bread; and when He had given thanks, He broke *it* and said, 'Take, eat; this is My body which is broken for you; do this in remembrance of Me.' In the same manner He also took the cup after supper, saying, 'This cup is the new covenant in My blood. This do, as often as you drink it, in remembrance of Me.' For as often as you eat this bread and drink this cup, you proclaim the Lord's death till He comes" (1 Corinthians 11:23-26).

Passover? Celebrate!